From the library of

SOPHENE

Published by Sophene 2022

The *History of the Tartars* by Het'um the Historian,
was originally written in the 14th century. First translated into English by
Robert Bedrosian in 1977 (revised and expanded in 2004).

A searchable, digital copy of the English translation can be accessed at:

https://archive.org/details/HetumTheHistoriansFlowerOfHistoriesOfTheEast

www.sophenebooks.com
www.sophenearmenianlibrary.com

ISBN-13: 978-1-925937-89-3

HET'UM THE HISTORIAN

HISTORY
OF THE
TARTARS

TRANSLATED BY
ROBERT BEDROSIAN

SOPHENE BOOKS
LOS ANGELES

CONTENTS

Translator's Preface ... xi

BOOK ONE

The Kingdom of Cathay ... 1
The Kingdom of Tars ... 3
The Kingdom of Turkestan ... 4
The Kingdom of Khwarazmia ... 5
The Kingdom of Komania ... 6
The Kingdom of India ... 8
The Kingdom of Persia ... 10
The Kingdom of Media ... 11
The Kingdom of Armenia ... 12
The Kingdom of Georgia ... 13
The Kingdom of Chaldea ... 15
The Kingdom of Mesopotamia ... 16
The Kingdom of the Land of the Turks ... 17
The Kingdom of the Country of Syria ... 19

BOOK TWO

The Lordship of the Saracens ... 23

BOOK THREE

The Land Where the Tartars First Lived ... 32
Chingiz-Khan, the First Emperor of the Tartars ... 36
Ogedei, the Second Emperor of the Tartars ... 39
Jinon-Khan, the Third Emperor of the Tartars ... 42
Ogedei's Eldest Son, Jochi ... 43
Ogedei's Second Son, Baiju ... 44
Yohaghata, Third Son of Ogedei ... 45
Mongke Khan, the Fourth Ruler of the Tartars ... 46

The Baptism of Mongke Khan	49
How Mongke-Khan's Brother, Hulegu, Wasted Assyria and Entered the Kingdom of Persia	50
How Hulegu Took the City of Baghdad and Did Away with the Caliph, Head of the Saracen Religion; the Death of the Caliph	51
Regarding the Persecution of the Saracens	52
How Hulegu Conquered the City of Antioch	53
The Taking of Damascus and the Holy Land as Far as the Egyptian Desert	54
Qubilai-Khan, Fifth Ruler of the Tartars	55
The Death of Hulegu and How the Sultan Took Back the Land of Syria and Egypt	57
Abagha, Son of Hulegu, Who Succeeded to the Lordship of His Father	58
How the Sultan of Egypt Defeated the King of Armenia, Capturing One of His Sons and Killing the Other	59
How Abagha Entered Egypt and Destroyed the Country of the Turks	61
The Poisoning of the Sultan of Egypt	62
How the Tartar General, Mangodan, Fled Due to Fear	63
Teguder, Hulegu's Second Son, Who Succeeded Abagha to the Throne	65
How Abagha's Son, Arghun, Became Lord of the Tartars After Teguder's Death	67
Arghun's Successor, Geikhatu	68
How Baidu, Lord of the Tartars, Died	69
How Arghun's Son, Ghazan, Seized the Lordship, and Concerning His Deeds	70
The Victory and the Division of the Booty	72
How the Traitor Qipchaq Returned the Country to the Sultan	74
The Great Injury Born by the Tartars in the Plain of Damascus from the Inundation of the Waters	76
How the Sultan made a Truce with the King of Armenia	79

Regarding the Division of My Book from the Beginning	80
T'amar-Khan, Sixth Ruler of the Tartars, His Authority and Lordship over Subjects	81
More on the Tartars' Religion and Customs	83
The Prerequisites for Starting a Battle	84
Affairs of the Kingdom of Egypt and the Sultan's Capabilities	85
The Authority of the Sultan in the Land of Syria	87
The Kingdom of Egypt and How It Changed Hands	88
How the City of Acre was Taken from the Christians	90
The Position and Circumstances of Egypt	92

BOOK FOUR

When is the Time to Start the War?	95
When They Should Go Into the Holy Land	96
How the Enemies of the Christian Faith were Reduced and Put Down	97
How Gharbanda, King of the Tartars, Offered to Go to the Holy Land with His Forces	98
Concerning the Enemy's Strengths and Weaknesses	99
The Names of the Nine Sultans Who Were Slain and Poisoned	100
Provision against the Sultan of Egypt	101
How Ambassadors Should be Sent to Gharbanda, a King of the Tartars, so that the Enemies Should Have Nothing Brought to Them	102
How the Sultan of Egypt Should Be Made Subject to the Christians and the Tartars	103
The General Passage	107

APPENDICES

Appendix I: Smbat's Letter to King Henry I of Cyprus 115
Appendix II: King Hetum's Trip to Mongke Khan 119
Appendix III: Rulers of Mongol Empires 127
Appendix IV: Rulers of Antioch, Cyprus, Jerusalem 131
Appendix V: Princes and Kings of Cilician Armenia 135

Index 139

TRANSLATOR'S PREFACE

The *History of the Tartars* first appeared in 1307 in the city of Poitiers. Dictated in French by the Cilician Armenian statesman and general, Het'um, and then translated into Latin the same year by his secretary, Nicholas Falcon, the work is contained in four books. Book I is a geographical survey of fourteen countries of the Far East, Central Asia, the Caucasus, Asia Minor, and parts of the Near East. Book II is a brief account of Muslim military history, including the rise of the Saljuqs and Khwarazmians. Book III, the longest, describes the early history of the Mongols, information on the Great Khans, the Il-Khans of Iran, and Mongol warfare in the Middle East, Central Asia and the Caucasus to ca. 1304. Book IV contains Het'um's suggestions to Pope Clement V (1305-14 on initiating a crusade to retake Jerusalem and parts of Cilician Armenia, Lebanon and Syria from Muslim powers, using the combined forces of the Europeans, Cilician Armenians and Mongols. Some scholars have suggested that Book IV was not part of the original French composition, but was added to the Latin translation and then translated into French and appended to the French text. Without Book IV, Het'um's work is an interesting account of Asian, Middle Eastern, and Mongol history and geography, to be categorized with accounts of 13th century European visitors to the East. With Book IV, Het'um's *History* enters the ranks of Crusader literature, but with the difference that its author, rather than being a pious and limited cleric, was instead a successful and influential general and tactician who had participated with his troops in numerous Mongol campaigns against the Mamluks.

Het'um, born sometime in the mid 1240s, was a son of prince Oshin, lord of Korikos in Cilician Armenia. Though biographical details of his early life are lacking, his family clearly enjoyed great influence in Cilicia. His father, Oshin, was the younger brother of King Het'um I (1226-69) and of the king-

TRANSLATOR'S PREFACE

dom's Constable, Smbat *Sparapet* (commander-in-chief of the army; d. 1276). Of the author's own children, several were also deeply involved in Cilician affairs of the late 13th century: Baudoin became governor of Tarsus; Constantine became Constable; Oshin became regent of Cilicia during the reign of Levon III (1305-07); and daughter Zabel (born 1282) was the wife of King Oshin (1307-20).

There is uncertainty about Het'um's official functions throughout the late 13th century. He states in chapter 46 of the *History* that he cherished the dream of retiring from political and military affairs and becoming a monk. However, it was not until 1305 that he accomplished this. Here, too, there is ambiguity, with some suggesting that Het'um was forced out of Cilicia after losing in a power struggle with his enemy, King Het'um II (1289-93, 1294-97, 1299-1307). The Cypriot chroniclers paint a very negative picture of Het'um's activities after he had become a canon regular of the Roman Catholic Praemonstratensian order. In their accounts, Het'um's aim was anything but religious. Rather, it was to promote the career of Amalric of Tyre and his own favorites in Cilicia; his visit to the papal court at Poitiers in 1306 was to enlist the Pope's support for Amalric's ambitions in Cyprus, and he attempted to bribe papal legates to achieve this. The Cypriot chroniclers also note that Het'um returned to Cyprus in 1308 and, within six days, had removed his cowl and departed for Cilician Armenia where he presumably resumed his political activities. His death has been placed between 1310 and 1320.

What sources did Het'um use in creating his *History*? In chapter 46, he himself characterizes them as written, oral, and personal (from 1263 on):

> *I, who wrote this book, know all that is in the third part in three ways. Events which transpired from the time of Chingiz-Khan, first emperor of the Tartars, to Monge-Khan, the fourth*

emperor, were taken from the histories of the Tartars. Events from Monge-Khan to the death of Hulegu, I heard from my honorable uncle King Het'um of Armenia who was present at all of them. With great diligence he retold them to his sons and nephews, and had us put it in writing for a remembrance. From the beginning of the reign of Abagha-Khan, son of Hulegu, to the third part of the book where the history of the Tartars ends, I speak as one who was present in person; and what I have seen I have recorded accurately.

In chapter 10 Het'um refers vaguely to the "histories of the kingdoms of Armenia and Georgia" for a confused story not known from any of them. In chapters 13 and 14 he references unidentified "histories of the eastern regions," which he followed in designating Trebizond as a district rather than a kingdom, and for the territorial divisions of Syria. Chapter 15 several times refers the reader to the histories of the crusader Godfrey of Bouillon (d. 1100). Chapter 17 mentions the "histories of the Tartars", one of which, perhaps, was Juvaini. Chapter 32 references a "chronicle of the Holy Land" which may be the same work as the "book of the conquests of the Holy Land" mentioned in chapter 52.

Het'um's uncles, Smbat and King Het'um I, would have been extremely rich and accessible oral sources. During the initial period of Mongol-Cilician contact, both had made the multi-year journey to the Far East: Smbat in 1247-51 and King Het'um I in 1254-55. Smbat described some of his observations in a letter in French to his brother-in-law Henry I of Cyprus (See Appendix 1).

TRANSLATOR'S PREFACE

King Het'um's journey, which our author describes briefly, also was described in detail by an eastern Armenian historian, Kirakos of Gandzak (see Appendix 2). Eastern Armenian and Cilician Armenian clerics would have been an invaluable source as well, since there were numerous Armenian clerics serving as translators at the stopping places en route to Mongolia and at the courts of the khans in Iran and Mongolia throughout the second half of the 13th century. The author himself appears to have visited the Caucasus (chapter 10), and states that he was present at the installment of two Mongol khans (chapter 16), though it is believed that he is referring to the Il-Khans of Iran rather than the Great Khans of Mongolia. Het'um, as a general, also participated in Mongol military campaigns in various parts of the Middle East for at least three decades (chapters 42, 44, 46).

Prior to the appearance of Het'um's *History* in 1307, western Europeans knew about the Mongols primarily from the accounts of clerical travelers to the Far East. Among this determined group were John of Plano Carpini and Brother Benedict the Pole (1245-47), Ascelin and Andrew of Longjumeau (1247-48), William of Rubruck (1253-55), and John of Monte Corvino (1289-1328). As papal envoys, their observations on the daily life of the Mongols and the details of their own harrowing journeys are priceless. However, their often ill-prepared travels were viewed with great suspicion by the Mongols, who found their stated aims puzzling. In any case, with the possible exception of John of Plano Carpini, the envoys' focus was primarily religious, a circumstance which led to many shocking and painful encounters with the shamanist reality of the Mongols, and to much unintended (and unappreciated) humor. A noteworthy exception was Marco Polo's *Travels* (1298). Written by an observant and energetic merchant who spent twenty years in the Orient, Polo's work was intended to inform and to entertain, which it continues to do. Intertwined with invaluable ethnographic and historical information is a considerable amount of fantasy, including Amazons, dog-headed men, fantastic plants and other marvels.

If Polo's aim was to write an entertaining best-seller, Het'um's aim was to start a war. There is no fantasy in Het'um's *History*. In the geographical section he describes the countries' borders, major cities, rivers, mountains, agriculture, exports, religions, and military capabilities. The historical portions (Books II and III) which are remarkable for their breadth, are generally accurate, though Het'um occasionally conflates similar battles fought in the same area, or similar legends (such as the two icons of Edessa), and occasionally, though rarely, is off a year or two in dating events. His shrewd and detailed battle plans in Book IV contain estimates of required troops and materiel; while the preconditions for starting any war, which he lays out in chapter 49, are still valid today. As Het'um had fought Muslim powers diplomatically and on the battlefield for most of his adult life, his work is characterized by a hatred and denigration of Islam and shows a concomitant tendency to emphasize (or overemphasize) Christian currents among the Mongols. This latter, perhaps, was a deliberate exaggeration to further interest or influence Pope Clement V, at whose request the work was written.

Filling a gap in Europe's knowledge of the Mongols, Het'um's *Flower of Histories of the East* quickly became a popular work and remained so for several hundred years. The large number of extant manuscripts and translations attest to this. Fifteen copies of the original French text and thirty-one copies of the Latin text have survived. In the mid 14th century, the Latin text was translated back into French twice, while a vernacular Spanish text appeared at the end of the century. Printed editions soon followed. The French text was published three times in the early 16th century, and editions of the Latin text appeared in 1529, 1532, 1537, 1555, and 1585. Between 1517 and 1520 Richard Pynson published *A Lytell Cronycle*, an English translation he made from the French. Translations also

TRANSLATOR'S PREFACE

were made into German (1534), Italian (1559, 1562), Spanish (1595), and Dutch (1563 and three times subsequently in the late 17th century). By this time, Het'um had become known as Hetoum/Hethum, Haiton/Hayton, Haithon/Haython, and Brother Anton. An Armenian edition was published by Awgerean[1], based on a Latin text. The only modern edition of the French and Latin versions appeared in 1906.[2] The Spanish text, with a study, was published by Wesley Robertson Long.[3]

In 1988, Glenn Burger published Hetoum, *A Lytell Cronycle,* Richard Pynson's translation (c. 1520) of *La Fleur des histoires de la terre d'Orient* (c. 1307).[4] This is a corrected Old English text based on several surviving manuscripts of *A Lytell Cronycle* accompanied by an extensive introduction, commentary, bibliography, textual notes, French-English variants, indices of proper names and places and a glossary (Old English to modern English). Burger's work is a fine piece of scholarship, without which the present edition would not have been attempted.

In 1977, while assembling material for a study of the Turco-Mongol invasions of the Caucasus, I made an English translation of Awgerean's text. It was through the Awgerean edition that Het'um's work became accessible to several generations of Armenists who, like myself, lacked the linguistic competence to deal with medieval forms of French, Latin, or English, and access to the original texts themselves. Unfortunately, Awgerean's edition has numerous shortcomings. There are a large number of typographical errors, some of which the editor of the 1951 reprint noted parenthetically. Moreover, there are problems of faulty translation. In a brief introduction, Awgerean himself lamented the poor quality of the Latin text he was working with. As a result, he occasionally summarized especially thorny passages, sometimes misinterpreting them. There are also omissions. Apparently Awgerean's Latin text lacked Book IV, since it is absent from his edition. Awgerean also relocated the colophon of Het'um's secretary, Nicholas

Falcon, which appears at the end of Book IV in other versions, to the front of Book I. In this colophon Nicholas Falcon claims that Het'um had dictated the book without using notes of any kind. If applied solely to Book IV, the claim is quite believable, since the battle plans in Book IV were Het'um's own. But if applied to the entirety of Books I, II, and III, as Awgerean's rearrangement implied, the claim is unbelievable. Last but not least, whether due to a poor text or poor eyesight, Awgerean (almost) consistently confused the lower-case Roman numeral l (50) with i (1), which affects many of the numbers provided. Thus, for example, where the French, Latin, and English texts give troop strengths of xl (40) thousand, Awgerean's edition has xi (11) thousand. Not surprisingly, among Armenists relying solely on Awgerean, Het'um and his *History* gained a notorious reputation for unreliability, even though the fault was Awgerean's and not Het'um's.[5,6]

The present edition, which is intended for the general reader, is a translation of the Awgerean text, corrected and expanded with passages from Burger, and including our modern English translation of Book IV.

For additional information and bibliography on Het'um and the various texts and translations, see Burger.[1] For a detailed study of the Mongol invasions, see Volume 5 of the Cambridge History of Iran;[7] for eastern Armenia in particular, see Bedrosian (especially Appendix C).[8] For Cilicia, see Der Nersessian[9] and Bournoutian.[10] Additional bibliography is available in Toumanoff.[11]

Robert Bedrosian
Long Branch, New Jersey, 2004

TRANSLATOR'S PREFACE
BIBLIOGRAPHY

1. Awgerean, M. (1951). *Het'um Patmich' Tatarac'*. Venice: San Lazzaro. (Original work published 1842).
2. Kohler, C. (1906). *Recueil des historiens des croisades. Documents arméniens, tome. II. Documents latins et français relatifs à l'Arménie*. Paris.
3. Long, W. R. (1934). *La Flor de las Ystorias de Orient*. Chicago.
4. Burger, G. (Ed.). (1988). *A Lytell Cronycle: Richard Pynson's Translation (c. 1520) of La Fleur des histoires de la terre d'Orient (c. 1307)*. University of Toronto Press.
5. Galstyan, A. (1958). On the question of the characterization of Hetum's History of the Tatars. *Teghekakir, 9*, 63-72.
6. Hakobyan, V. A. (1971). On the translation of the book History of the Tatars. *Lraber, 1*, 80-89.
7. Boyle, J. A. (1968). *The Cambridge History of Iran, Vol. 5*: The Saljuq and Mongol Periods. Cambridge University Press.
8. Bedrosian, R. (1979). *The Turco-Mongol invasions and the lords of Armenia in the 13-14th centuries*. Columbia University, New York, NY.
9. Der Nersessian, S. (1969). The Kingdom of Cilician Armenia. In K. M. Setton & R. L. Wolff (Eds.). *History of the Crsades, Volume II: The Later Crusades, 1189-1311*. (pp. 630-659). University of Wisconsin Press.
10. Bournoutian, A. A. (1997). Cilician Armenia. In R. G. Hovannisian (Ed.). *The Armenian People from Ancient to Modern Times, Volume I*. (pp. 273-291). St. Martin Press.
11. Toumanoff, C. (1966). Armenia and Georgia. In J. M. Hussey (Ed.) *The Cambridge Medieval History, Volume IV* (pp. 593-637). Cambridge University Press.

HET'UM THE HISTORIAN'S
HISTORY OF THE TARTARS

BOOK ONE

CHAPTER 1

THE KINGDOM OF CATHAY

The kingdom of Cathay is considered the richest and most noble realm in the world. Full of people and incalculable splendor, it is located by the shore of the Ocean sea. There are so many islands in the sea bordering it that no one knows their number, since no one has visited all of them. Yet as far as the foot of man has travelled thereabouts, countless luxuries, treasures, and wealth have been observed. Olive oil is an item which fetches a great price there and is much esteemed, and kings and grandees have kept it with great care as a major medicine.

There are numerous strange animals in the kingdom of Cathay, which I shall not mention. People there are creative and quite clever; and thus, they have little regard for the accomplishments of other people in all the arts and sciences. They claim that they themselves are the only ones to see with two eyes, while the Latins see with but one eye, and all other peoples are blind. And their word is confirmed by the fact that, generally, they regard other people as imbeciles. For such a quantity of varied and marvelous wares with indescribably delicate workmanship is brought from that kingdom, that no one is capable of matching such goods in the scales.

All the people in that kingdom are called Cathayans, and among them are many attractive men and women. But by and large, they have tiny eyes and are beardless by nature. These Cathayans have very beautiful letters, in some respects similar in beauty to Latin letters. It is difficult to describe the [religious] doctrines of the people of this kingdom. For some folk worship idols made out of metal; some worship cattle (since they work the land which brings forth wheat and other produce);

some worship gigantic trees; some, the natural elements; some, the stars. There are those who worship the sun and those who worship the moon. Yet others have no belief or doctrine and lead their lives like irrational beasts. Although they are full of genius with regard to making all sorts of material goods, no acquaintance with the spiritual exists among them.

[In warfare] the people of this country are very cowardly, and must be heavily armed. However, they are extremely skilled on the seas where they defeat their enemies more so than on land. They possess many types of weapons not found among other peoples. As for the money which this people uses, it is made of sedge, of square shape and bears the royal stamp, and it is based on this stamp that the money's value is determined, great or small. If the money becomes worn through age, they take it to the royal court and exchange it for fresh money. They make vessels and other ornaments out of gold and other metals.

Only in the west is Cathay bordered by another kingdom, that of Tars. In the north is the Belgean desert, and to the south are the aforementioned islands in the Ocean sea.

CHAPTER 2

THE KINGDOM OF TARS

There are three provinces in the kingdom of Tars and their respective lords are styled kings. The people thereabouts are called Eo'gur.[1] They have always been idolaters and at present still are, excepting the kin of those kings who came, guided by a vision of the Star to Bethlehem in Judea to worship the birth of the Lord. Even now one may find many grandees and nobles among the Tartars who are descended from that line, and who firmly hold the faith of Christ. The idol-worshippers in these parts are powerless in arms, but gifted and perceptive in studying the arts and sciences. They possess their own distinct alphabet. All the inhabitants of this kingdom refuse meat and wine and refuse to kill any living thing. Their cities are extremely agreeable, and they have numerous temples wherein they worship the idols. Wheat and other produce grow abundantly here. But they do not have wine, for they regard it as sinful to drink it, in no way differing from the Saracens. In the east the kingdom of Tars is bordered by the above-mentioned kingdom of Cathay; in the west, by Turkestan; in the north, by a desert; and in the south by an extremely rich province called Sune, located between the kingdom of India and Cathay. In this province enormous diamonds are found.

---

1 *Eo'gur:* Uighurs.

CHAPTER 3

THE KINGDOM OF TURKESTAN

In the east, the kingdom of Turkestan is bordered by the kingdom of Tars; in the west, by the kingdom of Persia; in the north, by the kingdom of Khwarazmia; in the south it stretches to the Indian desert. In this kingdom there are few good cities. There are extensive, rolling plains for herds. Thus, the greater part of the inhabitants are tent-dwelling herders, that is, they live in such houses which may be transported easily from place to place. The large city of this kingdom is called Okerra.[2] Little barley or wheat is harvested here. [The people] never use wine, instead drinking Kursam[3] and other light beverages which they make, and milk. They eat rice, millet, and meat. They are called Turks. Although they are Mohammedan, nonetheless, some of them have no faith or laws. They lack their own letters, instead employing the Arabic script in the city and army.

---

2 *Okerra:* Otrar.
3 *Kursam:* kumis.

CHAPTER 4

THE KINGDOM OF KHWARAZMIA

The kingdom of Khwarazmia is well endowed with good cities and villages and abundant population; for it is a fertile and temperate land. They harvest much wheat and other produce, but have little wine. This kingdom borders a desert the length of which stretches one hundred traveling days to the east; in the west, Khwarazmia reaches the Caspian Sea; in the north, it borders the kingdom of Komania;[4] and in the south, the kingdom of Turkestan, discussed above. The major city of the kingdom is called Khwarazme and the people, Khwarazmians. They are pagans, lacking writing or laws and are ferocious warriors. Amongst them are people called Koltink' [Soldains], possessing their own language and using Greek letters and the Greek rite. They take communion in accordance with the Greek ritual, and they obey the patriarch of Antioch.

---

4 *Komania:* Kumans/Ghuzz.

CHAPTER 5

THE KINGDOM OF KOMANIA

The kingdom of Komania is extremely large, but because of the intemperate climate, it is a difficult place for human habitation. During the winter, in places, it gets so cold that it is impossible for man or beast to live. Meanwhile, in the summer, in other places, it gets so hot that neither man nor beast can bear the heat or the flies. This kingdom is almost entirely plains, and on such lands neither trees nor other wood are found, except in gardens by a few cities. The people who dwell in tents on those plains burn animal dung in place of wood.

In the east, the kingdom of Komania is bordered by the kingdom of Khwarazmia and a desert; in the west, by the Great Sea[5] and a small sea called the sea of Reme;[6] in the north by the kingdom of Kassi;[7] in the south, it stretches to the huge river called Et'il.[8] Every year this river freezes, and sometimes it remains frozen year-round; and men, as well as beasts, go about on the ice as though walking on land. By the shores of this river grow some trees of low height. On the far side of the river dwell various and sundry peoples not counted among [the peoples of] the kingdom of Komania, but obedient to its king.

There are some who dwell close to Mount Caucasus, which is very lofty and awesome. The goshawks and other large birds and birds of prey born on that mountain are white in color. This mountain is set between two seas; for on the west is the Great [Black] Sea and on the east, the Caspian Sea which lacks an outlet to the Ocean. It is like a lake, but by reason of its size, is called a sea. Yet it is larger than any lake in the world, for it extends from the Caucasus mountain to the beginning of the

---

5 *Great Sea:* Black Sea.
6 *Reme:* Azov.
7 *Kassi:* Russia.
8 *Et'il:* Volga.

Persian kingdom, dividing the entire land of Asia into two parts. The part to the east is called deeper Asia,[9] while the part to the west is called greater Asia.[10] There are many excellent fish in the Caspian Sea, while buffaloes and numerous other wild animals are found in the vicinity. On the far side are many islands where birds' nests, especially falcons, and marlyons,[11] and other types of birds which are found there and nowhere else. The major city of the kingdom of Komania is called Sarai. In the past it was a noble and renowned city, but it was overthrown and almost completely destroyed by the Tartars who took it forcibly, as we shall relate below.

---

9   *deeper Asia:* Central Asia and the Far East.
10 *greater Asia:* Asia Minor, Iraq, and western Iran.
11 *marlyons:* merlins.

CHAPTER 6

THE KINGDOM OF INDIA

The kingdom of India stretches very far [south] into the Ocean, which there is called the Indian Sea. This kingdom borders the kingdom of Persia and stretches east to the district named Balazam.[12] Precious stones called *palays*[13] are found in that province. In the north is the long and large Indian desert where, they say, King Alexander[14] found numerous snakes and various sorts of animals. In this kingdom the Apostle Thomas preached the faith of Christ and converted many districts and peoples. However, because they are very distant from other lands and places where the Christian faith is held, their faith became quite weak. And there is but one city wherein Christians dwell, for the rest [of the population] by and large has completely abandoned Christianity.

Now there are numerous islands in the south along the coast. People inhabiting them are black and go about totally naked in the summers because of the heat. They foolishly worship idols. There are sources of pearls and gold and many varieties of spices on those islands, which people frequently bring to this country.

An island named Ceylon is located there and it has gems, rubies and sapphires in particular. The king of the island has a rare ruby, large and choice. At the coronation of the king, the latter holds that stone in his hand and circulates through the city mounted on a horse. Only after this [ceremony] do people obey him as king.

---

12 *Balazam:* Badakhshan.
13 *palays:* balas rubies.
14 *Alexander* the Great (d. 323 B.C.).

The land of India itself is like an island, surrounded by the aforementioned desert and the Ocean. Consequently, it is difficult for someone to enter by land save by way of the kingdom of Persia. Merchants who would enter that country first go to the city known as Hermes,[15] which the philosopher Hermes, as mayor, skillfully established, thence they pass along an arm of the sea until they arrive at the city of Kompak',[16] where green parrots may be found. And there are as many of those birds in that country as there are sparrows here. Merchants sell all kinds of wares in the harbor there. Should they want to advance farther, they may do so with no effort. The country lacks abundance of barley and wheat; instead, the inhabitants eat rice, milk, butter, and the fruits which grow there in plenty.

---

15 *Hermes:* Hormuz.
16 *Kompak':* Cambay.

CHAPTER 7

THE KINGDOM OF PERSIA

The kingdom of Persia is divided into two parts, though one king rules as common lord over both sections. The first part of the Persian land begins in the east, where it borders the kingdom of Turkestan, and stretches west to the great Phison River—the first of the four rivers flowing from the earthly Paradise. In the north, [the Persian kingdom] extends to the Caspian Sea; in the south, to the Indian desert. That land is entirely plains. There are two cities among others which are very large and opulent. One is called Poktara[17] and the other, Seonorgant.[18] The inhabitants of this kingdom are called Persians and have their own language. They live by trade and agriculture, but do not take up arms in battle. Previously they worshipped idols, and fire as the chief deity; however, when the faith of Mahmet conquered those parts, the people generally became Saracens, accepting the doctrine of Mahmet.

Now the other part [of the Persian kingdom] begins with the aforementioned Phison River and stretches west to the borders of the kingdom of Media, and partly to the borders of Greater Armenia. It extends north to the Caspian Sea and in the south [it borders one province of the realm of India and in some parts the ocean while another part borders] one of the districts of the Median kingdom. Two very large cities, Niwshapuh[19] and Spahan,[20] are located in that part of the kingdom. In religion and way of life, the people there resemble those [in the first part of the kingdom] whom we have described already.

---

17 *Poktara:* Bukhara.
18 *Seonorgant:* Samarqand.
19 *Niwshapuh:* Nishapur.
20 *Spahan:* Isfahan.

CHAPTER 8

THE KINGDOM OF MEDIA

The kingdom of Media is extremely long and narrow. In the east it borders the kingdom of Persia and, partly, the kingdom of Greater India. It extends westward to the kingdom of Chaldea; north to the kingdom of Greater Armenia; and south to the city of Ak'isum[21] by the Ocean. The large pearls found there circulate throughout the world.

In the Median kingdom there are great mountains and few plains. There are two districts [in the kingdom]. The people living in one of them are called Saracens; while those in the other district are called Kurds. The Median kingdom possesses two very great cities, one named Soraket[22] and the other Aworemon.[23] By law and faith they are Mohammedan and use the Arabic script. They are brave and powerful infantry bowmen.

---

21 *Ak'isum:* Qishm.
22 *Soraket:* Shiraz.
23 *Aworemon:* Kermanshah.

CHAPTER 9

THE KINGDOM OF ARMENIA

There are four kingdoms in the land of Armenia, but one monarch always holds the lordship. Lengthwise, the land of Armenia begins with the Persian kingdom and stretches west to the kingdom of the Turks. In breadth Armenia begins at the city of Darial, called the Iron Gate. This was constructed by King Alexander [the Great] because he did not want the various and sundry peoples living in the depths of Asia to enter Greater Asia without his command. This city was built at the narrow part of the Caspian Sea, and extended to the great Mount Caucasus.

Now in breadth, Armenia extends [from the same city] as far as the kingdom of Media. There are many great and rich cities in the kingdom of Armenia, but the most renowned is the city of Tabriz, which is more glorious than the rest. In Armenia, [the terrain consists of] lofty mountains, extensive plains, great rivers and lakes of both fresh and salt water with fish in abundance. The people inhabiting the land of Armenia are called by various names according to their districts and localities. They are valiant warriors, both mounted and on foot. In respect to armaments, they imitate the Tartars, under whose domination they have been for a long time. As for letters, they have [different sorts of alphabets], some Armenian and another besides, called Alo'ye'n.[24]

In Armenia there is one mountain, commonly called Ararat, which is taller than any other. And it was on the summit of this mountain that Noah's Ark first rested after the Flood. Now despite the fact that there is a great deal of snow on the mountain winter and summer, such that no one can climb it, nonetheless, on the mountain's summit something black is visible, which people say is the Ark.

---

24 The Old English text (hereafter, O.E.) renders Alcen (i.e., Aghuan).

CHAPTER 10

THE KINGDOM OF GEORGIA

The kingdom of Georgia begins in the east at the mountain called Alponis.[25] Many different peoples dwell there, and thus that district is named Alank'. The kingdom of Georgia extends to the west and north up to some lands in the kingdom of the Turks. Lengthwise it coasts the Great Sea.[26] In the south it borders the kingdom of Greater Armenia. The Georgian kingdom is divided into two parts: one called Georgia, and the other, Abkhazia. There were always two kings there, one of whom, the king of Georgia, fell under [the sway of] the Emperor of Asia. The other king, of Abkhazia, has many people and secure fortresses. Thus, neither the Emperor of Asia nor the Tartars were able to subjugate them.

There is a miraculous and strange place in the realm of Georgia which—had I not seen it with by own eyes—I would neither dare to speak about it nor to believe in it. But since I was there in person and saw it, I shall discuss it. There is a district named Hamshen in that area, its circumference being a three day's journey. And despite the district's extent, the place is so foggy and dark that no one can see anything. For no road goes through it. People in those parts say that one frequently hears the sounds of men bellowing, of cocks crowing, of horses neighing in the forest, and the murmuring of a river which flows thence. These are all regarded as trustworthy signs there that a settlement of people exists in the area. This much is true: in the histories of the kingdoms of Armenia and Georgia it may be read that a certain wicked Emperor Shaworeos,[27] an idolator and ferocious persecutor of Christians, one day ordered that all the inhabitants of Asia come and worship the idols.

---

25 *Alponis:* Mount Elbrus.
26 *Great Sea*: Black Sea.
27 *Emperor Shaworeos*: Shapuhr II (A.D. 309-79).

Those who ignored the command were to be burned with fire. Whereupon it transpired that some of the Christians chose martyrdom to worshipping the idols. Some chose to convert temporarily and, out of fear, worshipped the idols, so that they not be deprived of their lives and worldly goods. Meanwhile others took to the mountains and deserted places and somehow kept themselves alive. The group of the best Christians who lived in the Mughan plain thought to leave their belongings and to pass to Greece.[28] While they were so resolved, the [Persian] Emperor arose before them, ordering that those refusing to sacrifice to the idols should be pulled apart, limb by limb. Now the people cried out to the Lord Jesus Christ and, going by the straight path, they survived. However, the infidels have resided in that gloomy valley to the present. And then the Christians made a great cry to Our Lord God, and soon after came this great darkness that blinded the Emperor and all his men; and so the Christian men escaped, and the Emperor with his men tarried in the darkness. And they must stay there until the end of the world. So it is believed by everyone, and so it is related.

---

28   *Greece:* Byzantium.

CHAPTER 11

THE KINGDOM OF CHALDEA

The kingdom of Chaldea stretches from the Median mountains in the east to the great and ancient city of Nineveh, close to the Tigris River, the same city mentioned in the Bible. Nineveh is the city mentioned in the Holy Scriptures where the prophet Jonas was sent to preach at the command of God. Today it is a complete ruin; and, after regarding the folk who still dwell there, one needs confirmation to believe that Nineveh was once one of greatest cities in the world. In breadth, the kingdom of Chaldea stretches north to the city of Maragha and south to the Ocean. The major city of Chaldea, Baghdad, is commonly called Babylon as it has ever been known. It was to Babylon that Nebuchadnezzar led into captivity the sons of Israel from the holy city of Jerusalem.

There are many plains and few mountains in the kingdom of Chaldea, and few rivers pass through it. Some of the inhabitants of Chaldea are called Nestorians and belong to the heresy of Nestorius; they employ the Chaldean[29] alphabet. Other inhabitants use Arabic and are of the Mohammedan faith.

---

29 *Chaldean:* Syriac.

CHAPTER 12

THE KINGDOM OF MESOPOTAMIA

In the east the realm of Mesopotamia stretches from the great city of Mosul, built by the Tigris River, far westward to the Euphrates River and the city of Roha,[30] which was the city of Abgar's kingdom. It was to Abgar that the Veronica icon—which is now in Rome—was sent. And close to Urha is the land of Harran,[31] where Abraham once dwelled. The Lord commanded him to leave Harran and to pass to the Promised Land on the other side of the Euphrates River. Thus, Scripture is full of traditions about it. In Greek, this land is called Mesopotamia because it lies between two rivers of Paradise, the Tigris and the Euphrates.

In breadth the country stretches from one of the Armenian mountains called Sanson[32] south to the desert of Lesser Arabia. This land has numerous beneficent and agreeable plains. There are two very tall and fruitful mountains: one in the east called Siniat[33] and the other [in the west] called Lisson.[34] Few rivers flow through this country, thus the people drink water from wells and basins. There are some Christians among them, such as the Syrians and Armenians, while others are Saracen by law and religion. The Christian Armenians are valiant cavalrymen and infantrymen, while the Saracens and Syrians never raise arms, since they are craftsmen and tillers of the soil, and some, herders of flocks. However, in the place named Merdin there are some extremely skilled Saracen bowmen called Kurds.

---

30 *Roha:* Urha (Edessa).
31 *Harran:* Carrhae.
32 *Sanson:* Sasun (Sason).
33 *Siniat:* Mount Sinjar.
34 *Lisson:* Diyarbakir mountain range.

CHAPTER 13

THE KINGDOM OF THE LAND OF THE TURKS

The kingdom of the land of the Turks is extremely good and large, possessing mines of silver, gold, iron and copper, as well as an abundance of alum. Similarly, there is plentitude of all kinds of grains, fruit, and wine. Many types of animals are found there, especially choice horses. In the east [the kingdom] borders Greater Armenia and, in part, Georgia; while in the west it extends to the city of Satalia,[35] built by the Greek Sea.[36] In the north it borders no country but, for its whole expanse, coasts the shore of the Great Sea.[37] In the south it borders Lesser Armenia and a part of Cilicia while part of it stretches to the Greek Sea, facing the island of Cyprus. This land is called Greece by many peoples of the East, since formerly the Emperor of Greece held this country of the Turks as his own property and it was then governed by the Emperor's dukes and officials. But after the capture of the country by the Turks and their settlement in it, they selected a lord to rule over them and called him sultan, that is to say, king. Thereafter the land was called the country of the Turks.

There are many districts containing very large major cities in the kingdom of the Turks. In the district of Lycaonia, the renowned city of Konya, the largest city in the kingdom, is located. The second district, Cappadocia, contains the city of Caesarea of Greece. The third district, Isauria, contains the

---

35 *Satalia:* modern Adalia.
36 *Greek Sea:* Mediterranean Sea.
37 *Great Sea:* Black Sea.

ancient city of Seleucia. The fourth district, Phrygia, contains the city Zikia[38] of Greece. Fifth is the district of Kisitan[39] with its city, Ephesus. Sixth is Bithynia, with the city Nicea. Seventh is Pamphlagonia, where the city of Kinapolis[40] is located. Eighth is called Kenex[41] with the city of Trabzon. This district was a kingdom, though for a brief time only. For when the Turks conquered what became the kingdom of the Turks, they were unable to take the city of Trabzon and those areas around it, due to the security of the fortresses and to other defenses. So it remained under the authority of the Emperor of Constantinople who would send a duke or general there each year to see to the country's economy. However, it came to pass that one of the dukes or overseers of the place revolted and personally seized power in the country, proclaiming himself king. And so, the man who seized the country of Trabzon had himself styled Emperor.

The inhabitants of these parts are Greeks and they conduct the Greek [Orthodox] rite and use the Greek alphabet. We have placed Trabzon among the districts and not kingdoms, because the histories of the eastern regions so instruct us. In the country of the Turkish kingdom dwell four peoples: the Greeks, Armenians, Jacobites (who are Christians living by trade and agriculture), and the Turks, who are Saracens and who took the lordship of that country from the Greeks. Some of them live by trade and agriculture, residing in cities and villages, while others always live in the forests and plains, winter and summer, as herders of flocks. And they are very skilled bowmen.

---

38 *Zikia:* Laodicea.
39 *Kisitan:* Lydia.
40 *Kinapolis:* Kastamonu.
41 *Kenex:* Pontus.

CHAPTER 14

THE KINGDOM OF THE COUNTRY OF SYRIA

The realm of Syria stretches from the Euphrates River in the east to the city of Samos[42] in the west, located by the Greek Sea, where the Egyptian desert begins. In breadth the kingdom extends from the city of Beirut to the Krak of Montreal.[43] In the east it borders Mesopotamia; in the north, it partly borders Lesser Armenia and partly the kingdom of the Turks. In the southwest no kingdom borders it, since it is surrounded on two sides by the Greek Sea and the Arabian desert.

The kingdom of the land of Syria is divided into four parts or states which, in antiquity, usually were styled kingdoms because of their size and because kings resided in them. However, in the histories of the East they are called districts, not kingdoms. The first and chief district of the Syrian kingdom is named Sham. The noble city of Damascus was built in its midst. The second district is called Palestine and contains the Holy City of Jerusalem. The third district is named Antiochia and contains two great cities: Aleppo and Antioch. The fourth district is called Cilicia, and in it is the impregnable city of Tarsus where the venerable Apostle Paul was born. Cilicia is presently called Armenia, for after the enemies of the Christian faith took that country from the Greeks and held it a long while, the Armenians so labored that Cilicia was retaken from the infidels. The King of Armenia holds the lordship there now, by the grace of God.

---

42 O.E. text: "*Gasere*" (Gazette, Gaza).
43 *Krak of Montreal:* Ash-Shaubak.

Various peoples dwell in the country of Syria: Greeks, Armenians, Jacobites, Nestorians, and Saracens. Furthermore, there are other Christian peoples resident there, such as the Assyrians and the Maronites. The Assyrians who are more numerous than the Maronites follow the Greek rite and long since have been obedient to the Holy Roman Church. While they speak Arabic, the church service employs Greek letters. The Maronites follow the Jacobite rite, using the Arabic language and letters. They dwell near Mount Lebanon and in the Jerusalem area. They are skilled bowmen and live by farming.

It takes twenty travelling days to traverse the length of the Syrian kingdom, while the breadth requires five days and, in some places, less than that, because the Arabian desert and the Greek Sea intersect here and there.

BOOK TWO

CHAPTER 15

THE LORDSHIP OF THE SARACENS

As is known from the Gospel of Luke, at the time of the birth of Our Lord Jesus Christ, Caesar Augustus, Emperor of the Romans, held absolute lordship over the entire world. But subsequently, a certain Persian king named Xossorasat[44] became the first to rebel from the Roman empire and to have himself styled Emperor of Asia. He seized control of Persia, Media, Armenia and Chaldea, and his authority so increased that he entirely wrested those territories from the Roman Emperor by force. Persian rule over this territory lasted for three hundred and twenty-nine[45] years. Then the Saracens took the rule of Asia from them, as may be seen from the account which follows.

In 622 A.D.,[46] the Saracens entered the kingdom of Syria and, through warfare, took the extremely wealthy city of Damascus from the Greeks who had held it for a long time. In a brief period, they captured the kingdom of Syria. Thereafter they besieged the great city of Antioch, which the Greeks also held at the time. Heraclius Augustus, Emperor of the Roman realm, having heard about this, immediately sent a large Greek auxiliary force to defend the city against the Saracens. And as soon as the troops of Emperor Heraclius arrived on the plain called Possen, they clashed with the Saracens, in a terrible, frightful battle. But finally, the Saracens grew stronger. In that battle the multitude of the fallen was countless, and even today many bones are visible there. So those Greeks, holed up in the city in great dread, were forced to give Antioch to the Saracens by means of various treaties and oaths.

---

44 *Xossorasat:* Xosrov Anushirvan (531-79) or Aparvez (591-628).
45 O.E. text: *"three hundred"*.
46 O.E. text: *"632 A.D."*

From there the victors surged forward, entering the rich districts of Cilicia, Cappadocia, and Lycaeonia, and in a few days took them under their sway, for no one could resist their force. Thus, they began to puff up with immodesty, and organized a fleet of galleys and many other ships and set sail for Constantinople. First, they put in at Cyprus and took the great city of that kingdom, called Costance, where the grave of saint Barnabas the Apostle is located. The huge wealth of the city was looted and countless multitudes were taken captive. The place was razed to the ground such that it remained uninhabited thereafter. Then they took Rhodes and many other Roman islands, looted them, and took many captives.

Following these events, they came upon Constantinople and besieged that splendid city by land and sea. Now when the Christians saw such a host of the enemy, they were dumbstruck with terror and, in humility, sought mercy from the Lord. Behold, God answered their prayers. For despite the fact that it was summertime and the sea was undisturbed by waves, suddenly an awesome storm arose, causing all the enemy's galleys and ships to sink. And not one of them survived. When the remainder [of the enemy army] saw this, they quickly turned in flight. Now when the Christians saw that they had been saved by the mercy of Christ, with great joy they designated that day in the early [feast] calendar to the glory of the Savior, forever. And to the present, this day is celebrated with devout solemnity by Christians in those parts.

The Saracens temporarily ceased warring and rested. Thereafter, assembling a multitudinous force, they planned to attack the kingdom of Persia. First, they penetrated the kingdom of Mesopotamia, then they headed for the kingdom of Chaldea—which was under the lordship of the Persian king. It was unable to resist, and the Saracens vented all their wrath upon that country. Meanwhile the King of Persia, named Yazkert[47] terror-stricken that he might fall under the domination of the Saracens, sent ambassadors to the provinces and kingdoms

---

47 *Yazkert:* Yazdegerd III (d. 651).

lying around the Phison River,⁴⁸ and entreated them for aid, promising huge stipends and honors to whomever came. Some 6,000 men⁴⁹ called Turkmens assembled from the kingdom of Turkestan which was nearer to Persia, and set forth to help the King of Persia, crossing the Amu-Darya River. Wherever they went they observed the custom of taking along their women and children. As a result, they could not move quickly, rather they traveled a short distance each day. The Saracens who were in the kingdom of Chaldea which they had conquered, as was described above, suspected that if the forces of the Turks and the Persians came together, they themselves would be unable to work their will, and so they correctly planned to hurry to attack the King of Persia before any aid could reach him. Thus, the King of Persia, unable to avoid battle, came out against the Saracens with his people. At the battle which took place near the city of Marg⁵⁰ there was an intense struggle and countless warriors fell on both sides. But finally, the Persians took to flight and the Saracens bravely pursued. They killed the King of Persia, among others, enjoying this triumph in the year 632.

When the King of Persia had thus died, the sons of Hagar put the Persian kingdom and others under their yoke. They set up one state and elected for themselves a ruler from the line of Muhammad whom they called Caliph, and stipulated that his seat should be in the very wealthy city of Baghdad. As for the other kingdoms which the Saracens conquered, in each one they set up a lord whom they called sultan. Thereafter they took many other cities and districts and all of Greater Asia, but excluding the kingdom of Abkhazia in Georgia, and that district in the kingdom of Armenia commonly called Aloyen.⁵¹ These two provinces resisted the Saracens and never wanted to submit. And so all the local Christians whom the Saracens persecuted

---

48 *Phison River:* Oxus or Amu-Darya.
49 O.E. text: "*4,000 men*".
50 *Marg:* Qadesya?
51 *Aloyen* (O.E. text: Glausegardfordes): Aghuania (Caucasian Albania), or modern Artsakh (Nagorno-Karabakh).

by forcing them to follow the laws of Muhammad, found asylum and protection there.

We have some brief information to relate about those Turkmens mentioned above who planned to help the Persian king, information which will make their history, which follows, easier to understand. The Turkmens reached a country called Khurasan, and learned there that the King of Persia had been killed in battle. They still wanted to advance, but considered it wise to take refuge in Khurasan, figuring that they could hold and defend that area from the Saracens. The Saracens observed this and assembled many troops to conquer the Turkmens by all means. But when the Turkmens saw the limitless multitude of the Saracens, they were afraid to give battle. They sent emissaries to the Caliph, agreeing to surrender to his pleasure and command, and petitioning him to preserve them under his lordship.

This proposal pleased the Saracens. Thus, they received the Turkmens and settled them in another country—where there was no fear of rebellion—and imposed upon them an annual tax payable to the realm as well as many other obligations. Thus did the Turkmens remain in subjugation to the Saracens for a long time, while the kingdoms of Persia, Media, and Chaldea converted to the religion of Muhammad. After this, the Caliph summoned to him the elders of the Turkmens and beseeched them to adopt the laws and religion of Muhammad, and to strive to have the rest of the Turkmens do likewise, promising them favors and honors if they would agree.

Because the Turkmens had no laws, they readily accepted the Caliph's proposal and became Saracens, one and all. As time went on, they showed such zeal for the faith that the sixty-four peoples of the Turkmens adopted the religion of Muhammad. All the Turkmens converted to the faith of the Saracens, excepting only two peoples, who were separated from those who had converted. Thereafter the Saracens started to warm to the Turkmens and gave them honors and other good things.

Thus, they increased in riches and in numbers, for they knew how to deal with the Saracen lordship in a cunning fashion until they found the proper place and circumstances for rebellion. They forcibly wrested the lordship from the hands of the Saracens, as shall be seen below.

The Saracens ruled in Asia for 198 years[52] before losing its sovereignty. But there arose some disturbances among them which lasted for thirty years, to the point that sultans and other princes of the land who were supposed to obey the Caliph began to rebel from him. For this reason, the authority of the Saracens was greatly reduced. At the same time, the valiant Diogenes[53] sat as Emperor in Constantinople. He started attacking the Saracens bravely and forcefully, and captured back many cities and fortresses which had fallen to them in the days of Heraclius. Besides other places, he freed the city of Antioch and the fortified cities of Cilicia; and part of the kingdom of Mesopotamia was also returned to Christian rule. Other kingdoms of Asia remained under Saracen domination until the Turkmens ruled those places, as we shall now see.

By 1051 the Turkmens had greatly increased in wealth and population. Seeing that conflicts were multiplying among the Saracens, they thought that they could easily take the empire of Asia from them. So they elected a king and lord over themselves, for previously they never had any lord from their own people, either generally or locally. Their first lord was named Satug.[54] With this man as leader, they bravely attacked the Saracens and in a short time took the entire territory of Greater Asia. But in no way did they harass or burden the Caliph. However, when the Turkmens had captured the lordship of the land of Asia, the Caliph—more out of fear than affection—wished to please them in everything, and designated Saljuq as their lord, and ruler of all Asia.

---

52 O.E. text: "*428 years*".
53 *Diogenes:* Nicephorus II Phocas (963-69)?
54 *Satug*: Saluq.

After a short time had passed, Saljuq died. He was succeeded by one of his sons called Tughril. Tughril began to stir up war against the Emperor of Greece and captured many of his lands and fortresses. He dispatched one of his relations, named Artot,[55] against the kingdom of Mesopotamia and permitted him to do whatever damage he could against the Greeks. Thus, this same Artuq himself, with a great host, took the road to the city of Edessa, which was besieged and captured without trouble. Then he turned against other countries and places and put all of Mesopotamia under his sway. He established his seat in the city of Mardin and had everyone address him as Sultan.

Then Tughril, the ruler of Asia,[56] died and his son Alp Arslan [1063-72] succeeded him. He had a nephew named Sulaiman who was skilled in arms and had greatly served his father. Alp Arslan dispatched him with many troops to Cappadocia and allowed him to do whatever damage he could against the Greeks. So Sulaiman went and took many cities of [what later became] the kingdom of the Turks and cast its entire lordship under his sway, and had himself called Sultan. Then he changed his name, styling himself Sulaiman-Shah. And the histories of the passage [expedition] of Godfrey of Bouillon recall him, for he was the first to war against the Christians. And of these men histories make mention of Godfrey of Bouillon's passage, when he fought with the pilgrims [crusaders], and did them great harm before they could go through the lands of Turkey.

Subsequently Alp Arslan, ruler of the Turks, died. His son, Malik-Shah [1072-92], succeeded him. Malik-Shah sent Artuq, the Sultan of Mesopotamia, and Sulaiman, Sultan of the country of the Turks, to besiege the city of Antioch. They took it after a short while, since the city was quite large and there were few soldiers to defend it or resist the Saracens. In such a fashion, the Greeks were expelled from all of Asia by the enemies of Christianity.

---

55 *Artot:* ibn-Artuq.
56 O.E. text: *"king of Persia".*

After this Malik-Shah, ruler of the Turks, died leaving two sons. The elder son, Pelkiarux[57] succeeded to his father's authority. However, his more forceful brother seized most of the lordship. At the time that Godfrey of Bouillon crossed through the country of the Turks, Barkiyaruk was ruler of Persia and Sulaiman was Sultan of the country of the Turks. He frequently assaulted the Christians prior to their passage through Turkey. Now when the Christians had passed through the kingdom of the Turks, and had besieged the city of Antioch, the ruler of the Turks heard about it and sent one of his generals named Korpaghat[58] with countless multitudes of warriors to aid the city. However, before he could arrive, the Christians had already taken the city. [The Saracens] thereupon surrounded them on all sides, and thus the Christians, who had been the besiegers, were now the besieged. But the Christians came out of the city deployed in ranks and fronts and battled the Saracens, exhausting and destroying the whole lot of them like dust, by the grace of God. The fugitives fled to the kingdom of Persia only to find that their lord Barkiyaruk had died. His brother wanted to succeed him in holding the lordship. But some of his adversaries sprang upon him and cut him to pieces. Thereafter they were unable to unite in selecting an Emperor, or a general leader for themselves. Instead, they battled one another in discord.

When the Georgians[59] and the Armenians of Greater Armenia observed this, they boldly and bravely attacked the Turks, forcing them to flee from the entire principality [of Persia]. Thence they went with their women and children to settle in the land of the Turks and so the principality of the Sultan of that country was greatly strengthened until it was mightier than all [of its neighbors]. Until the coming of the Tartars, this kingdom was maintained in peace, but thereafter its tranquility was shattered, as we shall see.

---

57 *Pelkiarux*: Barkiyaruk, sultan of Persia (1094-1105).
58 *Korpaghat*: Ibn Said Kerboga (d.1102).
59 O.E. text: *"Greeks"*.

In the Khwarazmian kingdom dwelled a people skilled in arms who always lived in tents in the fields and were herders of flocks. These people learned that the Persian realm was kingless, lordless, and helpless and thought that it would be easy to capture. Therefore, they consulted amongst themselves and chose a leader and lord, named Jalal al-Din [d. 1231]. United, they entered the Persian kingdom, going as far as the city of Tabriz, meeting no resistance. Here they established their base and crowned their lord, that same Jalal al-Din, as Emperor of Asia. For they planned to conquer the other kingdoms of Asia as easily as the Persian kingdom, which they had found without a master.

The Khwarazmians gave themselves over to relaxation and diversion, and, filled with the greatness of the Persian kingdom, they swelled with pride. They went against the kingdom of the Turks, thinking to conquer it. But Ala al-Din,[60] Sultan of the Turks, gathered his forces together and went before the Khwarazmians at the entrance to his realm. An awesome battle took place between them, but at last the Khwarazmians turned in flight, losing their chief and Emperor as a casualty in the battle. They themselves narrowly escaped and assembled in the plain of Edessa to decide what to do next. They decided to enter the kingdom of Syria which at that time was ruled by a certain woman.[61] Therefore they assumed that it would be a simple matter to capture it. However, that noblewoman had her forces assemble at the city of Aleppo and resisted the Khwarazmians. The battle took place by the Euphrates River, and, once again, the Khwarazmians were defeated and fled as far as the Arabian desert. They crossed the Euphrates River by fort Kakaw,[62] entered the land of the Syrians and went as far as the district of Palestine in the kingdom of the Jerusalemites. Here they caused considerable damage to the Christians, as may be found in detail in the histories

---

60 *Ala al-Din:* Ala-ad-Din Kai Kobad, sultan of Rum (1219-37).
61 *a certain woman:* Safia Khatun.
62 *Kakaw:* Rakka.

about Godfrey of Bouillon. Yet after this, in a short period, the Khwarazmian people were reduced to nothing, because they refused to obey their own seniors and became fragmented into bands. Some of them went to the Sultan of Damascus, some to the Sultan of Homs, others to the Sultan of Hamah and yet others to the sultans of the kingdom of the Syrians—there were five Syrian sultans at that time—and served them as mercenaries.

Now when Vardat,[63] the leader of the Khwarazmians, saw himself so forsaken by his people, he went to the Sultan of Baghdad and put himself and his relations at the pleasure and command of the Sultan. The Sultan thus received the Khwarazmians gladly and divided them among his forces, not wanting them to remain together. He greatly honored the Khwarazmian prince, giving him very glorious gifts and income. And to this day, descendants of that prince are honored in Baghdad. The Sultan of Baghdad's principality was enlarged greatly by the Khwarazmians, although before their arrival it had been small and weak. But now the Khwarazmians had become divided, and thereafter never amounted to anything. Thus were the Khwarazmians destroyed. Shortly afterwards the Tartars began to rule Asia, as we shall narrate more fully below.

---

63 *Vardat:* Berke Khan.

BOOK THREE
CHAPTER 16

THE LAND WHERE THE TARTARS FIRST LIVED

The land where the Tartars first lived is located on the far side of the great Belgean Mountain,[64] mentioned in the History of Alexander. The Tartars lived in that province like brute beasts, possessing neither writing nor [religious] faith. They tended flocks of animals and moved from place to place searching for fodder for their herds. They were unskilled in arms, scorned by, and tributary to, everyone. Formerly there were many Tartar peoples, commonly known as Moghols. They so multiplied that they divided into seven main peoples who are considered the most venerable among them.

The first of the Tartar peoples is called Tartar after the district of their ancient habitation; the second, Tankut; the third, Kunat; the fourth, Ealis; the fifth, Sonik'; the sixth, Mongi; the seventh, Depat'.[65] As we said, these seven Tartar peoples were subject to their neighbors until it happened that a certain poor old man, a ditch digger, had this vision in his sleep: he saw a soldier, entirely white, handsome, and mounted on a white horse. The rider called him by his name, saying: "Chingiz, it is the will of immortal God that you become princely overseer of the Tartars and lord over the Mongol peoples. Through you they shall be freed from servitude to their neighbors a condition they have long endured, experiencing quarrels and exploitation from nearby lords. And the tax which you give to them shall in turn be taken from them." Chingiz was filled with great joy upon hearing this

---

64 Burqan Qaldun.
65 *Tankut* (Tangut), *Kunat* (Oirat), *Ealis* (Chelair), *Sonik'* (Sunit), *Mongi* (Merkit) and *Depat'* (Tibet).

message of God, and he related the vision he had seen to everyone. However, their leaders and grandees did not want to believe the veracity of the vision and some laughed at the old man. The following night these same leaders saw the white soldier and the same vision which old Chingiz had related to everyone. And they received the decree from immortal God to obey Chingiz and to make everyone obey his orders. Thus, those seven leaders and grandees of the seven Tartar peoples gathered in an assembly and agreed to obey Chingiz as their natural lord.

Then they set up his throne amongst them, spread out on the ground a very black sheepskin, and seated Chingiz upon it. The seven great leaders raised him and placed him on the throne with great joy and clamor, and called him Khan, the first Emperor, and honored him by kneeling before him, as Emperor and lord. Now regarding this ceremony which the Tartars held [for enthroning] their first Emperor and lord, and regarding the sheepskin, let no one be surprised. Perhaps they had no other attractive fabric or did not know how to make something better.

One could be surprised by [their behavior] in modern times, for despite the fact that these very Tartars possess many kingdoms and immeasurable wealth, since the lordship and riches of Asia are in their hands, and since they rule to the very borders of Hungary, nonetheless, in no way have they sought to alter their old ways and customs. This is especially true for the chiefs who, when enthroning an Emperor of the Tartars, entirely retain that arrangement which their ancestors used. I personally was present at the enthronement of two of their Emperors. But now let us return to our earlier narration.

Chingiz-Khan, who became Emperor by the general consent and will of all the Tartars, before undertaking anything, wanted to discover whether all the Tartars would obey him loyally. Therefore, he issued [three] decrees that all were to keep. The first decree was that all Tartars should believe in and obey immortal God, by Whose consent he himself had received the dignity of the kingship. The Tartars kept this first decree, for thereafter they began to call upon God, and to this day in all of their affairs, the Tartars call upon the name of the Lord. The second command [Chingiz] gave was that an overseer be set up over each group of ten men; one over 1000 men; and one over 10,000 men; and 10,000 soldiers were called a *tuman*. He decreed, further, that the seven leaders or generals who ruled over the seven Tartar peoples, forever renounce all degrees of honor which they had previously held, and do so for good.

Next, he issued a frightful and unbelievable decree, for he ordered each of those seven Tartar generals to bring his eldest son, and to behead him with his own hand. Although the command appeared inhuman and impious, no one dared to disobey, for they knew that [Chingiz] was lord through divine providence. Therefore, whatever order he gave, they fulfilled at once.

Once Chingiz-Khan had tested his people's resolve, and saw that they were ready to obey him to the point of death, he stipulated a day on which all should be ready to go to war. So the Tartars rode out against their close neighbors, and subjected them. Thus, those who formerly were their lords, now became their servants. Subsequently Chingiz-Khan surged forth against many other peoples and soon conquered them, for he accomplished everything with few soldiers, and he was successful in everything.

Once it came to pass that Chingiz-Khan was raiding, accompanied by only a few of his cavalry, and the foe arose before him with a multitude. During the clash, Chingiz-Khan defended himself but the horse he was riding was slain. As soon as the Tartars saw their lord fallen flat in battle, they despaired of salvation and turned to flight, saving themselves from the enemy. The latter speedily pursued the fugitives, unaware that the King was lying there on the ground. Then Chingiz-Khan sprang up and hid himself in the bushes, thereby eluding the danger of death. Those who returned to the plain from the fight began stripping the corpses and searching for people in hiding. And it happened that a bird, called an owl [or eagle] by many, came and perched on the bushes in which the Emperor was concealed. When the searchers saw that bird perched on the bushes, they reasoned that no one was there, and without looking further for the one they were seeking, left the place, saying to themselves that should someone have been concealed there, that bird would never have perched.

In the dark of night, Chingiz-Khan went to his own people, traveling by untrodden paths, out of fear of the enemy. And he narrated to them, in order and accurately, what had happened to him. Then the Tartars offered thanks to immortal God. As for that bird which seemed, after God, the liberator of Chingiz-Khan, it became so honored by them that whoever possessed a feather of it was considered fortunate. The Tartars wear that feather on their heads with great honor. I have mentioned this matter here to explain why it is that Tartars wear feathers on their heads.

Chingiz-Khan became the Emperor of all those districts on the far side of the Belgean Mountain, conquering them without problems. Matters continued this way until he saw another vision, as will be related below. Let no one be surprised that I have not placed dating in this part of the narration. Although I asked many people about such, I was unable to find anyone who could fully inform me about it. I believe that this is because the Tartars then were unfamiliar with accurate chronology, for they had no script. Thus, events and their dates passed by without being recorded by anyone, and so were forgotten.

CHAPTER 17

CHINGIZ-KHAN, FIRST EMPEROR OF THE TARTARS

After Chingiz-Khan had put under his sway all the kingdoms and districts near Belgean Mountain, he saw another vision one night. Once more the white warrior appeared and said to him: "Chingiz-Khan, it is the will of immortal God that you pass the Belgean Mountain and head westward, conquering kingdoms, districts and territories and placing many peoples under your domination. So that it will be believed that these words reflect the will of immortal God, arise and go with your people to Mount Belgean, to the spot where the sea borders it. There you shall descend, and make nine genuflections toward the East, worshipping immortal God. Then the All-Powerful Himself will show you the road by which you may cross the mountain." When Chingiz-Khan saw that vision, he arose with delight and feared nothing. Because the first vision had come true, he now had credence in other visions. Therefore, he quickly assembled his people from all parts and ordered them to follow him with their women, children, and all their belongings. They went to the place by the mountain where the sea was vast and deep and no through road or pass appeared. Chingiz-Khan quickly descended from his horse as immortal God had commanded—and so did his people—genuflecting nine times toward the East and requesting the help of omnipotent, immortal God, that He show them the road and passes by which to advance. They spent that night in prayer, and in the morning arose and saw that the sea had parted from the mountain by nine feet, leaving a broad road. The Tartars, one and all, were astounded by that sight and fervently offered thanks to immortal God. They traveled along the road which they found had opened before them and directed their course to the west.

However, as is found in the histories of the Tartars, after Chingiz-Khan and the Tartars crossed that mountain, they experienced the deprivations of hunger and thirst for some days. They found the land a desert and they were unable to drink the bitter and salty waters. So it remained until they sighted a pleasant land where all the necessities were abundantly available. Chingiz-Khan remained in that fertile land for many days. However, by the providence of God, he became gravely ill—so ill that recovery seemed hopeless. Thus Chingiz-Khan, Emperor of the Tartars, summoned his twelve sons before him and advised them always to be united and of one mind. And he taught them a lesson: he ordered that each of his sons bring an arrow apiece, and when they were all gathered together, he commanded the eldest to break the entire bundle if he could. He took the twelve arrows and attempted to rend them, but was unable. Then the bundle was given to the second son, then to the third, and to the rest, son by son, but none was able to do it. Then [Chingiz] ordered the youngest son to divide up the arrows individually and to break them one by one. And he easily broke all of them. Then Chingiz-Khan turned to his sons and said: "My sons, why was it that you were unable to break the arrows I gave you?" They replied: "Because, lord, they were very many altogether." "But why was it that your youngest brother was able to break them?" "Because, lord, they were divided up one by one." And Chingiz-Khan said: "Thus it is among you, for as long as you are of one heart and soul, your rule will always hold firm. But when you separate from each other, your lordship will quickly be turned to naught." Chingiz-Khan gave many other very good precepts which the Tartars preserved. In their language these are called the *yasax* of Chingiz-Khan, that is the statutes of Chingiz-Khan.

Subsequently, before dying, he set up the wisest and best of his sons, named Ogedei-Khan, as lord and inheritor of the empire. Having done this, Chingiz-Khan died in peace, and his son Ogedei was placed on the throne of his father's kingdom.

Before concluding this narration, we should note the extent to which Tartars revere the number nine. This is in remembrance of the nine genuflections which the white warrior had commanded them to make to immortal God on Mount Belgean, and the road of nine feet in width over which they passed. Thus, they consider that number to be lucky. Should someone want to present something to the lord of the Tartars, he must offer nine things if he wants his gift to find favor. If nine items are proffered, it is sufficient for that gift to be regarded as fortunate and good. The Tartars observe this custom to the present day.

CHAPTER 18

OGEDEI, SECOND EMPEROR OF THE TARTARS

Ogedei-Khan, who succeeded his father turned out to be a robust and wise man. The Tartars liked him, unanimously showing loyalty and obedience to him. Now Ogedei-Khan wondered in what manner he could conquer all of Asia. First, he wanted to assay the strength of the kings of Asia and fight with the most powerful. For he thought that he would easily overcome the rest if he conquered the mightiest. He selected a brave captain for this named Gebesabada[66] and sent 10,000 cavalry troops with him and commanded them to enter the lands of Asia and view the state and condition of these lands; and if they found any mighty lord whom they were unable to resist, they should turn back. What Ogedei-Khan commanded was accomplished, for the captain with his 10,000 Tartars, suddenly entered the lands of Asia. There he took cities and lands, because the inhabitants were caught unawares and were unable to make ready for battle or defend themselves. [The Tartars] killed all the men of arms, but they did no harm to the people. They took horse, harness, food and all other things that they needed and continued on until they came to the mountain of Cocas.[67] Because of this mountain, no one can pass from the interior of Asia to Greater Asia without the consent of the people of a city that King Alexander fortified on a narrow sea which borders the mountain of the Caucasus. This city was taken by the 10,000 Tartars in such manner that its inhabitants had no time to defend themselves. When they took the city and everything therein, they put all the men and women to the sword and then broke down all of the city's walls, so

---

66 *Gebesabada* (from the O.E. text): Chormaghun?
67 *Cocas:* Caucasus.

that when they came back again, they would find no barrier against them. This city in antiquity was called Alexander, but now it is called the Iron Gate. News of the Tartar's arrival spread throughout all the countries and lands. As a result, the King of Georgia, named Ynaims[68] assembled his troops and came against the Tartars, fighting them in the Morgam[69] plain. The battle lasted for a long while, but in the end the Georgians were forced to flee. The Tartars continued on until they came to a city in Turkey called Arseon[70] when they learned that the Sultan of Turkey was nearby and that he had assembled his host together. Therefore, the Tartars did not dare advance farther, and, seeing that they could not beat the Sultan of Turkey, they returned by another route to their lord, whom they found in the city called Amelect.[71] They informed him of all they had done and learned in the land of Asia.

As a result of this, Ogedei-Khan selected a certain brave and wise general, named Payton[72] and entrusted him with 30,000 Tartar soldiers, termed *damak* or reconnaissance troops. He commanded them to go over the same road which the 10,000 had traversed, not tarrying until they reached the country of the kingdom of the Turks; and then, if possible, to try to resist the Sultan of the country of the Turks, who was reputed to be the mightiest of all the princes of Asia. But should it happen that they be unable to oppose him, they should not engage in battle, but instead make camp in some good country and notify one of his sons nearby to send them help, and then they could safely begin a battle.

---

68 *Ynaims:* Iwane Zakarean (Mxargrdzeli).
69 *Morgam:* Mughan.
70 *Arseon:* Erzurum.
71 *Amelect:* Amalic.
72 *Payton:* Baiju.

When Baiju with the 30,000 soldiers reached the realm of the Turks, travelling day by day, he learned that the sultan from whom the first Tartars had fled, had already died, and that his son named Kiadati,[73] had succeeded him. When [Ghiyath al-Din] heard about the coming of the Tartars, he was horrified and summoned as many mercenary troops as he could from foreigners and from the Latins. He had in his service, among others, a group of Latins led by two commanders, one named Yohannes Liminad[74] from Cyprus, and the other, Vonip'akios[75] from Venice. [The Turkish Sultan] also sent to neighboring sultans promising favors and gifts to anyone who came. And thus, gathering a great multitude of warriors, he went to the place where the Tartars were encamped. However, the Tartars were in no way perturbed. Instead, they valiantly waged war at Konsedrak.[76] In the end the Tartars were the victors and the Turks were defeated. In this way the Tartars captured the kingdom of the country of the Turks in the the year of our Lord 1244.

---

73 *Kiadati:* Ghiyath al-Din Kai Khusrau.
74 *Liminad:* Iohnn de la Limynate.
75 *Vonip'akios:* Boniface de Moulins.
76 *Konsedrak:* Kose-Dagh.

CHAPTER 19

JINON-KHAN,[77] THIRD EMPEROR OF THE TARTARS

After a short while Ogedei-Khan died [1241]. His kingdom was [eventually] inherited by his son, Guyuk,[78] who was short-lived. He was succeeded by one of his extremely powerful relations, named Mango[79] who put numerous territories under his sway. Gaining confidence, he crossed the Cathay sea and tried to take an island.[80] But while he was besieging the island, men from that place—who are extremely shrewd and clever—sent other men to secretly dive into the sea. They persisted at their task underneath the boat which Mongke was crossing in, suspected by no one, until by evening they created holes in the vessel. The ship went down to the deep, and Mongke-Khan drowned.

Now the Tartars who were with him turned back and elected Mongke's brother, Qubilai-Khan, as their lord [1262]. Qubilai-Khan ruled the Tartars for forty-two years. He converted to Christianity and built the city called Eons[81] in the kingdom of Cathay, a city said to be greater than Rome. In this city Qubilai-Khan ruled as Emperor to the last day of his life [d.1294].

Let us now pause in this account of the Tartar [Great] Khans and say something about the three sons of Ogedei-Khan, and about Hulegu and his successors.

---

77 *Jinon-Khan:* Guyuk-Khan.
78 *Guyuk*: Guyuk-Khan (1246-48).
79 *Mango*: Mongke-Khan (1251-59).
80 *an island:* Japan?
81 *Eons:* Beijing.

CHAPTER 20

OGEDEI'S ELDEST SON, JOCHI

Jochi, eldest son of Ogedei-Khan, invaded westward with a great host of cavalry, which his father had given him. He found fertile, pleasant, and rich territories there, and conquered the kingdom of Turkestan and lesser Persia, extending his lordship to the Phison River. He always remained with his band, which grew in possessions and numbers. To the present the successors of Jochi hold the lordship in those parts. Two brothers now rule that province, one named Kapar[82] and the other Doaks.[83] Having divided between themselves the land and the retainers, they dwell in peace and comfort.

---

82 *Kapar:* Chapar.
83 Doaks: Toqta.

CHAPTER 21

OGEDEI-KHAN'S SECOND SON, BAIJU

Baiju, the second son of Ogedei-Khan, went with those Tartar troops given him by his father and invaded the northern regions, reaching as far as the kingdom of Komania. The Komans who had many armed men, resisted the Tartars, thinking to protect their country. But in the end, they were defeated and went as fugitives as far as the kingdom of Hungary. To this day there are many Komans living there. Now after Baiju had expelled all the Komans from the kingdom of Komania, he passed to the kingdom of Russia, and subjugated that as well. And he conquered the country of the Kacar[84] and the kingdom of the Bulgars, and traversed the road over which the Komans had fled, reaching as far as the kingdom of Hungary. After this, the Tartars headed toward the kingdom of Germany until they reached a river which flows through the duchy of Austria. The Tartars planned to cross a bridge at the place, but the duke of Austria and other neighbors fortified the approaches to the bridge, preventing the Tartars from using it. Enraged by this, Baiju commanded all to cross and he himself went first into the river, subjecting his own person and his people to the danger of death. Before reaching the other shore, the horses gave out due to the breadth of the river and the strength of the current. Thus, Baiju drowned, together with a huge multitude of his followers. When those who had not yet entered the water saw this, struck with dread and shame, they returned in great sorrow to the kingdom of Russia and Komania and held them, as was said. Thereafter the Tartars did not go to the country of Germany. The heirs of Baiju hold the lordship of the realms of Khwarezmia, Komania and Russia; and the current lord is Chaghatai, third son of Ogedei-Khan. They dwell in peace and quiet.

---

84 *Kacar*: Possbly, Khazars.

CHAPTER 22

YOHAGHATA,[85] THIRD SON OF OGEDEI

Ogedei-Khan's third son, Chaghatai, invaded southward to lesser India with the Tartars given him by his father. He encountered many deserts, mountains, and unwatered barren lands until he was unable to proceed through those districts; for not only had he lost a multitude of men, but many animals as well. He then turned westward and after many trials reached his brother, Jochi, to whom he related the episodes of his journey. Now Jochi was sympathetic to his brother and humanely gave him part of the lands which he and his people had conquered. Thereafter those two brothers always lived together, and to this day their heirs dwell there, with the successors of the younger honoring the successors of the elder. Multiplying in their territories, they live in peace and tranquility. The current, living heir of Jochi is named Paraxi.[86]

---

85 *Yohagata*: Chaghatai.
86 *Paraxi*: Boraq.

CHAPTER 23

MONGKE-KHAN, FOURTH RULER OF THE TARTARS

In A.D. 1253 when lord Het'um, King of the Armenians, observed that the Tartars had completely subjugated all the kingdoms, districts, and territories up to the realm of the Turks, he consulted with his advisors and resolved to go in person to the King of the Tartars, to more easily obtain his favor and friendship, and to try to arrange a peace treaty with him. But first he sent baron Smbat, Constable of the Armenian kingdom, his brother, to obtain a decree of safe conduct for his journey. Thus Smbat, the King's brother, went to the Tartar Khan [in Karakorum, 1247] to graciously arrange the affairs of his patron. Four years later he returned to the Armenians [1251] to relate what he had seen and heard. Then the King of the Armenians [in 1254] went in secret so that he would not be recognized in the country of the Turks which he had to traverse. And as God willed it, the Tartar general who had defeated the Sultan of the Turks graciously received the Armenian King and had him conducted as far as the kingdom of [Greater] Armenia and to the Iron Gate. Thence other Tartar commanders accompanied him to Ameghek[87] where Mongke, Khan of the Tatars, resided. Mongke received him honorably and gave him great gifts and favors.

Now after some days had passed, the King of the Armenians beseeched the Khan regarding the peace treaty and other matters he desired. With the consent of the Khan, the King of the Armenians put [seven] requests before him. First, he urged the Khan to convert to Christianity and to accept baptism together with his people; second, he requested that eternal peace and friendship be established between them between the Tartars and the Christians; third, that it be possible to construct

---
87 *Ameghek*: Amelic, southeast of Lake Balkash.

Christian churches in all of the Tartar countries and that the Armenians be freed from taxes and other burdens that in all the lands that the Tartars had conquered and would conquer, the Christians—priests, clerks, and all religious persons—should be free of all taxes; fourth, that the Holy Land and the Holy Sepulcher be wrested from the Turks[88] and given to the Christians; fifth, that the Caliph in Baghdad, the head of the [Muslim] religion, be done away with [that he would command the Tartars in Turkey to help in the destruction of the city of Baghdad and the Caliph (the chief and teacher of the false faith of Mahmet); sixth, that all the Tartars stationed close to the realm of Armenia come to his aid when requested; seventh, that all the districts of the land of Armenians which the Turks had conquered be returned to him. The seventh request was that all the lands that the Saracens had taken that had belonged to the realm of Armenia and had since come into the Tartars' hands, be freely restored to him; and also, that all the lands he might conquer from the Saracens he might hold in peace without any dispute from the Tartars.

When the Tartar Khan had consulted with his princes and grandees, he replied to the King of Armenia: "I accept your requests. I shall accept baptism and adopt the Christian religion and show concern that all of my subjects do likewise, without, however, any coercion. Regarding the second request, let there be eternal peace between us, an alliance covering both offensive and defensive operations. The second request we will that perpetual peace and love be established among the Christians and the Tartars; but we will that you pledge that the Christians will hold good peace and true love toward us as we shall do toward them. Similarly we wish that all Christian churches, clergy and laity, enjoy freedom, and that no one harass the Armenians. And we will that all Christian churches, priests, clerks and all other persons, of whatever persuasion they be, secular or religious persons, shall be free and delivered of all taxes, and also,

---

88 O.E. text: "*Saracens*".

they shall be defended from all manner of hurt both of body and goods. Were it possible, we should like to revere the Holy Land in person; however, being occupied with other matters, we are sending our brother Hulegu to take it and return the Holy Land to the Christians. As for doing away with the Caliph of Baghdad, we entrust that task to Baiju, commander of the Tartars, and to his people residing in the realm of the Turks and thereabouts. The Tartars shall aid the Armenians in everything, and those lands which belonged to the Armenians should be returned to them without delay. We shall command our brother Halcon[89] to go with you to accomplish this deed, and shall deliver the Holy Land from the Saracens and restore it to the Christians; and we shall send our command to Baiju and to the other Tartars in Turkey and to the others that are in those countries that they shall obey our brother Halcon. And he shall go to take the city of Baghdad, and destroy the Caliph as our mortal enemy. We command furthermore, as a special favor, that all fortresses and country which we capture should be given to the Armenian King for the defense of the land of Armenia. We grant with good will that all the lands which the King of Armenia requested should be restored to him and we command our brother Halcon that he yield to him all the lands that were of his lordship; and moreover, we give him all the lands that he may conquer against the Saracens, and of our special favor, we give him all the castles near his land.

---

89 *Halcon*: Hulegu.

CHAPTER 24

THE BAPTISM OF MONGKE-KHAN

Mongke, after accepting the requests of the Armenian King with charitable munificence, had himself baptized by the chancellor of the Armenian kingdom who was a bishop. His house, and numerous other esteemed and noble men and women were baptized with him. Then he appointed troops to accompany his brother, Hulegu, in aiding the Holy Land. Now Hulegu and the King of Armenia travelled together with a great company of troops, until they had crossed the Phison River. Hulegu conquered the entire realm of Persia in three months' time.[90] He went as far as the kingdom of the Assassins. These people were faithless and lived without laws, and would kill themselves on the direction of their king. And they took all the lands and countries up to where the Assassins dwelled. These are men without any faith or belief except what their lord, called the Old Man of the Mountain, taught them; and they are so obedient to their lord that they put themselves to death at his command. They had a fortress named Dikaton[91] which was supplied with all the necessities, and extremely secure. Hulegu ordered one of his generals to besiege it with his Tartar troops and not depart until he had taken it. After twenty-seven years, the place was taken because of the privations caused by the siege. It was at this place when Hulegu had begun the siege that the King of Armenia, honored with many gifts by Hulegu, returned to his kingdom after three and a half years.

---

90   O.E. text: "*six months' time.*".
91   *Dikaton*: Possibly, Gerdkuh.

CHAPTER 25

HOW MONGKE-KHAN'S BROTHER, HULEGU, WASTED ASSYRIA AND ENTERED THE KINGDOM OF PERSIA

Hulegu, after seeing to what was necessary and proper for the preservation of the kingdom of Persia, went to a district in the land called Sotlok'.[92] There he gave himself over to recreation and rest for the entire summer. But at the coming of winter, he besieged the city of Baghdad where the head and teacher of the Muhammedan religion lived. Hulegu called up 30,000 Tartar troops who were in the country of the Turks. After assembling his people from all parts, he attacked that city and quickly took it. When he had gathered his host, he had the city of Baghdad assailed on all sides, until they took it by force; and they put to the sword the men and women they encountered. The Caliph was arrested and led before Hulegu; and they found such astounding wealth there that it was truly a wonder to behold. The city of Baghdad was taken in the year 1258.

---

92 *Sotlok'*: Soloch, plain of Hamadan.

CHAPTER 26

HOW HULEGU TOOK THE CITY OF BAGHDAD AND DID AWAY WITH THE CALIPH, HEAD OF THE SARACEN RELIGION; THE DEATH OF THE CALIPH

Once Hulegu had done what he willed with the city of Baghdad, he commanded that the Caliph be brought before him and had all his treasures put in front of him. Hulegu asked him: "Do you realize that all the things you see were yours?" And the Caliph replied: "Yes." Then Hulegu reproached him: "How is it that with all this wealth you did not have mercenary troops and call your neighbors to preserve yourself and your country from the might of the Tartars?" The Caliph replied: "I thought that my people would be sufficient." Then Hulegu said to him: "You were called Caliph, head of all those holding the religion of Mahmet, yet you choked on your wealth. Now such a great leader should be fed on no other food. This huge amount of wealth is the food which you so loved and kept with insatiable greed." Having said this, Hulegu ordered that the Caliph be placed in a room and that pearls and gold be set before him, so that he eat of them as much as he pleased. He decreed that no other food or drink be given to him. Thus did that wretched, greedy, covetous man dismally end his life. Thereafter no caliph resided in Baghdad.

CHAPTER 27

REGARDING THE PERSECUTION OF SARACENS

After conquering Baghdad and the surrounding areas, Hulegu divided the districts among his generals and administrators as he saw fit. He decreed that kindness be shown to Christians everywhere and that the maintenance of fortresses and cities be entrusted to them, while the Saracens were thrown into the meanest servitude.

The wife of Hulegu, named Dukos saron,[93] was a Christian descended from the line of those kings who had come from the East, guided by the Star, to be present at the birth of the Lord. This woman, an extremely devout Christian, caused all the Christian churches there to be rebuilt, and all the Saracen mosques demolished. All their religious celebrations in honor of the head of the faith [Muhammad] were prevented, and thus were the Saracens put into servitude from which they did not emerge for some time thereafter.

---

93 *Dukos saron*: Dokuz khatun.

CHAPTER 28

HOW HULEGU CONQUERED THE CITY OF ANTIOCH

Then Hulegu relaxed for a year in the city of Edessa. He sent to the King of Armenia for him to come to him with his troops, for he planned to go to the Holy Land to deliver it to the Christians. King Het'um set out with 12,000 cavalry and 40,000 infantry and went to Hulegu. For in this period, the realm of Armenia was prospering, so that [Het'um] had 12,000 horsemen and 12,000 infantry; and I saw that in my day. Het'um said to [Hulegu]: "Your Excellency, the Sultan of Aleppo holds sway over the entire country of Syria and the city of Jerusalem is located in that kingdom. Therefore, if you capture the main city of Aleppo first, you will be lord of the entire country of Syria." Hulegu accepted the advice and ordered that Aleppo be besieged. The city was very strong, fortified with walls, heavily populated and wealthy. Hulegu courageously attacked it, making use of underground passages, with machinery called mules, with bowmen, catapults, and various other sorts of weapons. Despite the fact that the city seemed impregnable, he took it in nine days, discovering an unbelievable amount of treasure there. In the center of the city was a fortress which he took with rock-hurling devices, after twelve days.[94] So Aleppo was taken and after that, the entire realm of Syria in the year 1260.

---

94 O.E. text: *"eleven days"*.

CHAPTER 29

THE TAKING OF DAMASCUS AND THE HOLY LAND AS FAR AS THE EGYPTIAN DESERT

After this, Hulegu took the city of Damascus together with the sons and wife of the Sultan of Aleppo. The latter went to Hulegu seeking their return and also mercy, but his hopes were frustrated. For Hulegu sent him with his wife and children to the kingdom of Persia, so that Syria would remain tranquil. Hulegu gave to the King of Armenia a large part of the booty and numerous fortresses close to his kingdom. The Armenian King had these fortified as he chose.

Subsequently, Hulegu sent presents to sent for the duke of Antioch[95] who was a relative[96] of the King of Armenia, and ordered that all the districts of his kingdom which the Saracens had held be returned to him. He also bestowed many other favors on him. Having put these affairs in order, he immediately wanted to go against Jerusalem to return it to the Christians. But just then, bad tidings from a reliable source reached him regarding the death of his brother and the fact that the throne of the Tartar Khanate was vacant and that the lords wanted to make him Emperor. As soon as he heard this [news about his brother's death, [Hulegu] fell into deep sorrow and advanced no farther. Instead, he made his way east, leaving his son named Abagha in Tabriz. He appointed a general named Kit-Bugha and gave him 10,00 troops, to hold the kingdom of the country of Syria, to take Jerusalem, and return it to the Christians.

---

95 Bohemond VI.
96 O.E. text: *"son-in-law"*.

CHAPTER 30

QUBILAI-KHAN, FIFTH RULER OF THE TARTARS

When Hulegu reached the land of Persia, he received news that the nobility and grandees had already seated his brother Qubilai on the throne of the Tartar Khanate. Once Hulegu heard this he went no farther, but returned again to Tabriz where he had left his son, household, and servants. While in Tabriz he learned that Partat[97] was coming with great preparation into his lands. Hulegu immediately assembled the entire multitude of his people and went against his adversaries on a certain frozen river. There a ferocious battle took place. But from the weight of the multitude of soldiers and horses, the ice gave way and 30,000 Tartars drowned from both sides. The remaining two armies turned back greatly saddened over their losses.

Meanwhile Kit-Bugha, whom Hulegu had left in Syria and Palestine, conducted the affairs of those regions peacefully and greatly loved the Christians. For he, too, was a descendant of those three kings who had come to adore the nativity of the Lord. Kit-Bugha was interested in returning the Holy Land to the Christians but the devil fomented discord between him and the Christians of those parts. For in the country of Tepel Fordis[98] in the lordship of the Sidonites were numerous villages and districts where the Saracens lived and provided the Tartars with set taxes. It happened that some men from Sidon and Belfort gathered together, went to the Saracens' villages and fields, looted them, killed many Saracens and took others into captivity together with a great deal of livestock. A certain nephew of Kit-Bugha who resided there, taking along but few cavalry, pursued the Christians who had done these things to

---

97 *Partat:* Berke.
98 *Tepel Fordis:* Belfort.

tell them on his uncle's behalf to leave the booty. But some of the Christians attacked and killed him and some other Tartars. When Kit-Bugha learned of this, he immediately took the city of the Sidon and destroyed most of the walls [and killed as many Christians as he found. But the people of Sidon fled to an island, and only a few were slain. Thereafter the Tartars no longer trusted the Christians, nor the Christians the Tartars. But later the Tartars were expelled from the country of Syria, as I shall relate below.

CHAPTER 31

THE DEATH OF HULEGU AND HOW THE SULTAN TOOK BACK THE LAND OF SYRIA AND EGYPT

While Hulegu was battling with Berke, as was described above, the Sultan of Egypt[99] with his assembled troops arose from Egypt and went to Henialek[100] in Palestine and began warring with the Tartar general Kit-Bugha [A.D. 1260]. Kit-Bugha was slain there while those Tartars who narrowly escaped made their way to [Cilician] Armenia. Thereafter the country of Syria once again fell under the domination of the Saracens, excluding a few cities on the coast which the Christians held. Learning about this, Hulegu assembled his troops and sent to the King of Armenia, the King of Georgia, and other eastern Christians in Syria, that they come in readiness to battle the Sultan of Egypt. When he himself had assembled his soldiers, he fell ill and died after fifteen days. This was a great loss, since the Holy Land would not be captured again. His son, Abagha, succeeded him, and at his request his uncle, Qubilai-Khan, confirmed him in his father's lordship in the year 1264.

---

99 *Sultan of Egypt*: Kutuz.
100 *Henialek*: Haymelot, Ain Jalut.

CHAPTER 32

ABAGHA, SON OF HULEGU, WHO SUCCEEDED TO THE LORDSHIP OF HIS FATHER

Abagha was a wise and capable man who wielded authority successfully. However, he did not want to become a Christian, as his father had. Instead, he was an idolater and always stirred up wars with his neighbors. This meant that he was unable to defeat the Sultan of Egypt, whose power, therefore, increased. The Sultan of Egypt also did a clever thing; for he sent his messengers to the Tartars in the realms of Komania and Russia, making peace and friendship with them and ordaining that if Abagha came into Egypt, they would invade his lands and make war on him. Consequently, Abagha never attempted to attack the kingdom of Egypt. Thus, the Sultan of Egypt was easily able to conquer the country of Syria, and thus did the Christians lose dominion over Antioch and many other fortresses in Syria as is written in the chronicle book of the Holy Land.

CHAPTER 33

HOW THE SULTAN OF EGYPT DEFEATED THE KING OF ARMENIA, CAPTURING ONE OF HIS SONS AND KILLING THE OTHER

Following this, the Sultan of Egypt, Bntuxtar,[101] grew so strong that he also destroyed the kingdom of [Cilician] Armenia. It happened that the King of Armenia had gone to the Tartars with a large force, and the Sultan of Egypt had learned about this. So he sent his troops to attack the kingdom of Armenia. Now when the Armenian King's sons learned about the coming of the Saracens, they assembled all who could bear arms, went against the Egyptians, and started to battle successfully. But in the end, the Armenian force was defeated, and one of the King's sons was taken captive while the other was killed in battle. The Saracens raided throughout the kingdom of Armenia, polluting all the plains with the sword and taking immeasurable spoils, which was an enormous loss for the Christians. Thereafter, the might of the enemy increased, while that of the King of Armenia declined greatly. Although the King always tried to destroy the power of the Saracens, and many times endeavored to incite Abagha and the Tartars against them, Abagha repeatedly refused, since he was warring with neighbors. Thus forsaken, the Armenian King sent to the Sultan of Egypt to negotiate with him so that his son be freed from prison. The Sultan agreed on the condition that his own friend, Sankolasar,[102] whom the Tartars were holding in captivity, be returned to him and that the fortresses of the city of Aleppo be handed over to him. Thus, the Sultan returned the King's son and received back his friend, and the King turned over

---

101 *Bntuxtar*: al-Malik Rukn-ad-Din Bibars Bunduqdar (Baibars).
102 *Sankolasar*: Sonqor al-Achqar.

to the Sultan the fortress of Tempezak'[103] and at the Sultan's request had two other fortresses demolished. After these events, King Het'um, of blessed memory, who had reigned for fifteen years, entrusted the kingdom to his son, lord Levon, who had been freed from captivity in Egypt. Het'um himself forswore this vainglorious life and became a cleric, styled Makar. After a short while he died peacefully in the year 1270.

---

103 *Tempezak'*: Darbsak.

CHAPTER 34

HOW ABAGHA ENTERED EGYPT AND DESTROYED THE COUNTRY OF THE TURKS

The Armenian King, Levon, ruled wisely and with an alert mind, beloved by his own people and by the Tartars. With all his heart he labored to destroy the Saracens. Now it came to pass that Abagha made peace with his neighbors, with whom he had been inimical for a long time. Then the Sultan of Egypt entered the country of the Turks, killed many Tartars and conquered many villages and districts. A certain Saracen, named P'arwana, who was in the country of the Turks and was head of the Tartars, had revolted from Abagha and was trying to ruin the Tartars or cause them to desert. When Abagha heard about this, he arrived there in fifteen days. When the Sultan of Egypt heard of the coming of the Tartars, he wanted to flee the land of the Turks, but was unable. For the Tartars had set out quickly and attacked the rearmost wing of the army at a place called Basplang,[104] at the approaches of Egypt. The Tartars attacked and seized two thousand Saracen cavalry and many goods. They also seized five thousand Kurdish families dwelling in that district. However, when Abagha reached the borders of the country of Egypt, he did not want to advance farther because of the heat, for that district was extremely warm. Furthermore, the Tartars and their beasts which had come a very far distance in a hurry, were unable to bear the toil and heat. So Abagha returned to the country of the Turks, and he routed and destroyed all the rebellious places and those which had surrendered to the Sultan. As for the traitor P'arwana and his cohorts, Abagha had him cut to bits, according to Tartar custom. He then ordered that at every meal some of the flesh of the traitor P'arwana be set out. And Abagha and the nobility ate of this. Such was the manner in which King Abagha wreaked vengeance on the traitor P'arwana.

---

104 *Basplang:* Lepas Blanc (the pass of Aqchai Bogazi).

CHAPTER 35

THE POISONING OF THE SULTAN OF EGYPT

Having worked his will against the country of the Turks, and when the Tartars were loaded with the loot and riches that they had taken from the rebel Saracens, Abagha summoned the King of Armenia and offered the realm of the Turks to him, for [Levon] and his father had always been loyal to the Tartars. The wise and judicious King of Armenia thanked him for the gift, but rejected it on the grounds that he was unable to direct two kingdoms. For the Sultan of Egypt was extremely powerful and was plotting the destruction of the kingdom of Armenia. And the Armenian King advised Abagha to set in order the affairs of the realm of the Turks before departing so that no Saracen would be able to establish lordship there and so that there would remain no threat of rebellion. Abagha accepted the King's advice and forbade Saracens from holding the lordship in the country of the Turks. When this was done, the King of Armenia beseeched him regarding freeing the Holy Land from the infidels. Abagha so promised, simultaneously advising the Armenian King to send emissaries to the Pope and to the orthodox kings regarding this matter. Abagha ordered the King of Armenia to send to the Pope and to the other kings and lords of the Christians of the West, that they should come or send their men to help the Holy Land and to keep the lands and cities that they should conquer. Then the King of Armenia departed and returned to his land and sent his messengers to the Pope and to the kings of the West. Abagha arranged what was necessary and returned to the kingdom of K'orasten[105] where he had left his family. Bntuxtar, who had done such wicked things to the Tartars, was poisoned to death in Damascus. The Christians of the East were delighted by this, while the Saracens were saddened by the loss of the brave sultan. Bntuxtar was succeeded by his son, Melik-zade.[106] After a short while he was expelled, and Ershi became Sultan.[107]

---

105 *K'orasten*: Khurasan.
106 *Melik-zade:* al-Malik as Said Nasir-ad-din Muhammed (1277-79).
107 *Ershi:* al-Mansur Saif-ad-Din Kalawun al-Elfy (1279-90).

CHAPTER 36

HOW THE TARTAR GENERAL, MANGODAN, FLED DUE TO FEAR

When Abagha was planning to war against the Sultan of Egypt, he sent his brother, Mangodan,[108] to the country of Syria with 30,000 Tartar troops, to occupy it and give it to the Christians, and he himself [Abagha] would follow after. If the Sultan came against them, they should bravely fight with him. And if the Sultan dared not come to battle, he commanded that they should occupy the lands and cities and deliver them into the hands of the Christians to keep. Abagha also notified the King of Armenia. The latter arrived at once with his many troops, and they entered the country of Syria together, looting everywhere as far as the city of Homs, known to many at the time as Semel,[109] located in the center of Syria. Before they arrived at the city, there was a plain on which the Sultan had amassed his forces to oppose the Tartars. The Saracens waged a fierce battle with the Tartars and Christians. The King of Armenia headed the right wing. He attacked the left wing of the Sultan of Egypt's army and put it to flight as far as the city of Hams, and even farther.[110] Then Almax,[111] with his Tartar troops, trounced the other side and sent the Saracens fleeing to the city of Dara.[112] But Mangu Timur—never having seen battle—encountered some Saracens called Vitin,[113] and was terrified, stopped operations, and abandoned the field of victory leaving the King of Armenia and the [Georgian] constable who had gone in pursuit of their enemies.

Now when the Sultan, who thought everything was lost, saw the field of battle empty and completely deserted, he went up onto a mountain, fortified it with his 4,000 troops, and captured the place. But when the Armenian King returned from

---

108 *Mangodan:* Mangu Timur, d.1282.
109 *Semel:* la Chalemelle.
110 O.E. text: *"and three leagues beyond."*
111 *Almax:* Alinaq, a Georgian general.
112 *Dara:* Qara.
113 *Vitin:* Bedouins.

dispersing the enemy, and did not find Mangu Timur, he was astonished and went back after him. Similarly, Alinaq who had also fought the Saracens, waited two days for Mangu Timur—for he knew that the latter had set out—then he hastened to go after him, leaving off his conquering. They rode as far as the banks of the Euphrates, but could not overtake Mangu Timur. After this, the Tartars returned to their place. Now the King of Armenia and his troops suffered greatly on that journey, for from the length of the trip and scarcity of goods, the horses were thoroughly worn out and were unable to advance. Thus, going along separated from one another via untrodden places, they were mercilessly attacked by the Saracens of the area. Most of the army was lost and almost all the vassals. This unfortunate event occurred in the year 1282.

When Abagha-Khan was informed about all of this, he gathered his multitudinous troops and had them prepare to enter the realm of Egypt. But just then some Saracen came to the kingdom of Persia and gave many bribes to some of Abagha's intimate servants and got them to agree to administer poison to Abagha and his brother, which they did. Both of them died after eight days, the truth of the matter being confused by those very villains. This poisoning occurred in the year 1282.

CHAPTER 37

TEGUDER, HULEGU'S SECOND SON, WHO SUCCEEDED ABAGHA ON THE THRONE

Following the death of Abagha, the Tartars assembled and set up Abagha's brother, Teguder, as their lord. In his youth, Teguder had been baptized Nicholaus, but later in life, he cleaved to the Saracens whom he loved, and wanted to be styled Muhammad-Khan. He tried by all means to convert the Tartars to the faith of Muhammad, gave gifts and honors to those whom he did not dare to force; as a result, countless Tartars became Saracens. Then this son of the devil ordered that all Christian churches be destroyed, and that Christians not dare to preach the laws or doctrines of Christ any longer. He had Muhammad's laws and doctrines preached publicly. He had the Christians banished, and he had the Christian churches of Tabriz totally destroyed. He sent to the Sultan of Egypt and established a peace treaty with him, and vowed to force all Christians in his lordship to become Saracens, or else have them beheaded. Whereupon the Saracens filled with every joy, while the Christians, were overcome with sadness and dread. And there was nothing they could do but call upon the mercy of God to help them, for they experienced very great persecution.

Furthermore, Muhammad-Khan himself sent to the King of Armenia and the King of Georgia and to other Christians ordering them to come before him at once. However, the Christians resolutely decided to die willingly rather than to submit to the impious order [to convert], for there was no other sentiment. While the faithful were so anguished, behold, God, Who never abandons those who place their hopes in Him, gave solace to all the Christians. For that Muhammad-Khan's brother, and his nephew, Arghun, who were opposed to such wicked deeds, went to Qubilai, Great Khan of the Tartars, and informed him that Muhammad-Khan had forsaken the way of their forbears, become a Saracen, and was taking the rest of the Tartars along with him.

As soon as Qubilai-Khan heard this, he became extremely agitated, and sent an order to Muhammad-Khan to pull back and desist from such wickedness or else he would come against him. But Muhammad-Khan ignored the Khan's command and, filled with anger and rage, killed his own brother. Wanting to slay Arghun as well, he went against him with a huge force. Arghun, unable to resist, fled to the mountains and holed up in a secure fortress. Muhammad-Khan came and besieged this with his troops until Arghun surrendered to him, on condition that he and his lordship be left unharmed. Muhammad-Khan entrusted Arghun to his Constable [Alinaq] and his grandees and returned to Tabriz, where he had left his sons and women, ordering the Constable and his confidants to kill Arghun and to send the head to him.

But the righteous judgement of God, Who preserves the innocent and those who strive for true faith, saw to it that one righteous liberator exist among the impious murderers. This was a brave man, [Buqa], motivated by compassion, who had been nourished by Abagha, Arghun's father. During the night, he raised his sword and struck down the Constable and his co-conspirators. Then he set up Arghun—who was saved from death—as lord and governor of all. Whereupon some through affection and some through fear recognized him as their lord. When this was accomplished, [Arghun] hastened after Muhammad-Khan, seized him, and had him cut to pieces. And so perished this enemy of the faith and the faithful, after a lengthy, unjust misrule of the country in the second year of his reign [1284].

CHAPTER 38

HOW ABAGHA'S SON, ARGHUN, BECAME LORD OF THE TARTARS AFTER TEGUDER'S DEATH

In 1284 A.D., Arghun sent ambassadors to the Great Khan of the Tartars to relate all that had transpired. The Great Khan was much pleased at this and sent some senior members of his house to establish the lordship of Arghun. Thereafter he was honored by everyone and called Khan. The handsome Arghun loved the Christians and looked after his lordship bravely and wisely. And he restored the churches ruined by Muhammad-Khan. Therefore, the kings of Armenia and Georgia, together with other Christians, went and beseeched him that the Holy Land be taken through his plan and aid. He consulted about this and then replied that he would do whatever was possible according to their wishes, after making peace with his neighbors.

Although he wanted to fulfill his promise, he died in the fourth year of his reign.[114] He was succeeded by his brother, a useless man named Rheghayid,[115] as we shall explain.

---

114 This should be the 7th year of his reign (1284-91).
115 *Rheghayid*: Geikhatu.

CHAPTER 39

ARGHUN'S SUCCESSOR, GEIKHATU

After Arghun-Khan's death in 1288,[116] his brother Geikhatu succeeded him,[117] a man who had no laws or faith and was also powerless in arms. Giving himself up entirely to debauchery and sin, he led the life of a dumb beast, a slave to the belly. He reigned for six loathsome years and was held contemptible in the eyes of others until, at last, he was strangled[118] by his nobles. After his death, his relative Payton [Baidu] seized the lordship. This Baidu was a believer in Christ, and a just man. And he granted the Christians many favors. However, he was not to live long.

---

116 O.E. text: *"1289"*.
117 *Geikhatu*, 1291-95.
118 O.E. text: *"drowned"*.

CHAPTER 40

HOW BAIDU, LORD OF THE TARTARS, DIED

After the death of Geikhatku, Baidu reigned. He built many Christian churches, and stopped the preaching of the faith of Muhammad among the Tartars. But because many had already converted, they were displeased by that command. Thus, they sent secret messengers to Ghazan, Arghun's son, promising him the lordship if he would deny Christ, which he did. Now Baidu assembled his hosts and went to arrest Ghazan. But when he reached the place of battle, he was deserted by all the believers in Muhammad. He fled and died in flight.

CHAPTER 41

HOW ARGHUN'S SON, GHAZAN, SEIZED THE LORDSHIP, AND CONCERNING HIS DEEDS

After the death of Baidu, Ghazan became lord of the Tartars,[119] and true to his promise, he was hostile toward Christians. However, after establishing his authority, he began honoring and being affectionate to Christians, and he did away with those people who had lured him to the Saracens' faith, and put to death all those who had advised him to harm the Christians]. Then he ordered his Tartars to raise arms, and he called up the King of Armenia, the King of Georgia and other Christians, for he planned to war against the Sultan of Egypt.

In spring Ghazan-Khan went to Baghdad, where he assembled his troops and prepared to go against the city of Homs in the center of Syria, where the Sultan of Egypt, Melik'nasr, and his troops awaited him. Ghazan-Khan learned that the Sultan was coming to fight him, and therefore he did not delay by taking castles and towns, but went straight to the place where the Sultan was, encamping a day's journey distant in a meadow with plenty of grass, where he ordered his men to rest with their horses, so that they might recuperate from the fast pace of the march. With Ghazan was a Saracen servant of the Sultan named Galpak'[120] who had been ruler of Damascus and had fled from the Sultan out of fear. Ghazan-Khan had received Qipchaq affectionately and trusted him greatly. Qipchaq was, however, a traitor, for he [secretly] advised the Sultan to quickly commence battle since Ghazan's horses were very fatigued. The Sultan followed this advice and came in a hurry. Ghazan's spies had informed him of this, and telling [the few]

---

119 *Ghazan*: 1295-1304.
120 *Galpak'*: Qipchaq.

troops [at hand] to battle courageously, they went before the enemy. Ghazan went against the Saracens more bravely than a lion. When Ghazan-Khan realized that he could not fight, and that his men could not reach him in time, he stayed where he was. He ordered his men to dismount from their horses and to form themselves into a wall and to shoot arrows at the enemy coming furiously against them. In this fashion the Tartars, united, shot arrows and downed many enemy horses, while those Saracens who were coming behind [the advance-guard] stumbled [on the horses]. Thus, from that multitude of Saracens only a few escaped alive. Many Saracens were left mortally wounded by the arrows, and died.

When the Sultan heard about this, he hastily drew back; meanwhile Ghazan, informed of this development, ordered his men to mount and to courageously attack the enemy. He himself went into battle first with the small band of men he had with him, until all his commanders could join the battle, and commenced killing the enemy. The Tartars battled from sunrise until noon. Thereupon the Sultan, unable to resist the bold bravery of Ghazan, turned to flight, and all the Saracens with him. Ghazan pursued, killing the enemy until the darkness of night. So severe was the blow dealt to the Saracens that the country filled up with corpses. After the battle that night Ghazan rested in joy and delight in a place called Caner[121] because of the victory due to God's aid. This occurred in A.D. 1301 on Wednesday, before the feast of the Birth of the Lord.

---

121 *Caner:* Rahit.

CHAPTER 42

THE VICTORY AND THE DIVISION OF THE BOOTY

After this Ghazan ordered the King of Armenia and a general of the Tartars, named Mugha [Moulai], to go with 11,000 cavalry[122] in pursuit of the Sultan of Egypt as far as the desert twelve days distant from the site of the battle. [Ghazan] commanded that they should await his arrival in the country of Cassore.[123] The King of Armenia and Moulai, with 40,000 Tartars, departed and went after the Sultan; and they killed as many Saracens as they could. After three days, the King of Armenia was called back by Ghazan, for he wanted to lay siege to the city of Hames,[124] and Moulai undertook to pursue the enemy. Now the Sultan, travelling night and day mounted on fast horses, guided by some Bedouins, miserably entered Babylon[125] without any troops, while the other [defeated] Saracens fled wherever they could. A great multitude of them fled on the route to Tripoli where they were mercilessly cut down by Christians living in the mountains of Lebanon.

When the Armenian King returned to Ghazan, he learned that the city of Homs, had surrendered to Ghazan with all the treasure and they marveled greatly that the Sultan and his men had brought along so much treasure with them, for a fight. The incalculable wealth they found was divided generously by Ghazan amongst his men, thereby greatly enriching them. I, brother Het'um, saw all of this with my own eyes, since I was there. I, Brother Het'um, was present at all the great encounters that the Tartars had with the Saracens, from the time of Hulegu on, but I never heard tell of any lord of the Tartars

---

122 O.E. text: *"40,000 cavalry"*.
123 *Cassore:* Gaza.
124 O.E. text: *"Homs"*.
125 *Babylon*: Not the Babylon of Mesopotamia, but Fustat in Egypt.

who did so great a deed in two days as Ghazan did. For on the first day of the battle, Ghazan, with a small company of men, proved himself against the Sultan and a great number of his men. It was miraculous that Ghazan, a man short in stature and of ugly mien, on one day destroyed the enemy and on the next day generously divided up all the wealth, keeping for himself only a dagger and a leather purse containing Egyptian writings.

And because Ghazan is of our own time, we must speak of him at greater length than the others; for the Sultan who was defeated by Ghazan is still living. Moreover, all who delay the passage to the Holy Land may derive good lessons from [this account]. After five,[126] days of relaxation, Ghazan went directly to Damascus unbeknownst to the horrified Damascenes. They resolved to send gifts and the keys of the city to Ghazan, requesting mercy. Ghazan humanely accepted and commanded that essentials for the needs of the army be brought. And he promised not to destroy the city but to keep it for the needs of his chamber. Ghazan himself pitched his tent by the banks of the Damascus River, preventing anyone from damaging the city. The Damascenes sent many gifts and a full supply of provisions. Ghazan remained [near Damascus] for fourteen,[127] days, there being besides 10,000,[128] men in Ghakk'ar,[129] awaiting the arrival of Ghazan.

---

126 O.E. text: *"some"*.
127 O.E. text: *"many"*.
128 O.E. text: *"40,000"*.
129 O.E. text: *"Gaza, with Moulai"*.

CHAPTER 43

HOW THE TRAITOR QIPCHAQ RETURNED THE COUNTRY TO THE SULTAN

Just then news reached Ghazan that his relation Baidu had invaded Persia and had caused Ghazan great damage. Now to prevent him from doing further damage, Ghazan thought to return to his own [people]. He therefore ordered Got'luz,[130] to remain in Syria to protect the country and he commanded Moulai and the other Tartars with him in Gaza to obey Qutlugh-Shah whom he was leaving in his place; then he appointed overseers for cities, entrusting the city of Damascus to Qipchaq. Ghazan did not realize that Qipchaq was a traitor. He summoned the King of Armenia and acquainted him with what he had ordered Qutlugh-Shah, that all the districts which to that time the Christians had seized, were to be given back to them and he would help with their fortification. Ghazan said: "We have delivered the land of Syria to you, for the Christians to hold. If they[131] come, we have left an order with Qutlugh-Shah that he shall deliver the Holy Land to the Christians, and that he should give advice and help to make the lands [prosper] again."

Having arranged these matters, Ghazan entered Mesopotamia. When he was near the Euphrates River, he sent an order to Qutlugh-Shah for him to leave Moulai with 20,000 Tartars, and to hasten to him with the rest. Qutlugh-Shah did so and Moulai stayed behind to hold Syria. But on the instigation of Qipchaq, Moulai passed to the Jerusalem area to the place called Kawr[132] to find fodder for

---

130 *Got'luz:* Qutlugh-Shah.
131 *they:* the Crusaders?
132 *Kawr:* Ghur or Ghur-al-Ourdun (valley of the Jordan).

his horses and other essentials. When summer arrived, Qipchaq sent messengers to the Sultan of Egypt, telling him to come to Damascus, and saying that he would give him Damascus and other places that the Tartars held in the country of Syria. The Sultan accepted this promise and in turn promised Qipchaq that if he remained true to his word, he would give him in perpetuity the lordship of Damascus, a part of his treasure, and his sister in marriage.

After a short while Qipchaq caused all the territories to rebel, for he knew that other Tartars would be unable to come and help, since their horses could not go on expeditions in that heat. When Moulai saw this, he was unable to offer resistance because of his lack of troops, so he turned to Mesopotamia where he found Ghazan and informed him about what had happened. Now when winter came, he assembled a force and sent Qutlugh-Shah back with 30,000 Tartar cavalry, ordering that the King of Armenia and other Christians be summoned as soon as he reached Antioch. When Ghazan arrived with a large army the realm of Syria would be entered. Qutlugh-Shah implemented all the orders. The King of Armenia and his troops came to the island of Anterad,[133] as did Christians of the kingdom of Cyprus. Also present was the lord of Tyre,[134] brother of the King of Cyprus,[135] with troops of the Orders of Templars and Hospitallers. When all of them were ready, news arrived that Ghazan was ill, so gravely ill that there was no hope of curing him. Therefore Qutlugh-Shah returned to Ghazan, the King returned to his country, and the Christians, who had come to the island of Ruad, returned to Cyprus. Thus, the matter of taking the Holy Land was abandoned. This occurred in 1301.

---

133 *Anterad:* Aradus (Arwad).
134 *lord of Tyre:* Amalric.
135 *King of Cyprus:* King Henry II (d.1310).

CHAPTER 44

THE GREAT INJURY BORN BY THE TARTARS IN THE PLAIN OF DAMASCUS FROM THE INUNDATION OF THE WATERS

In the year 1303, Ghazan assembled an extremely large army by the Euphrates River, planning to enter the country of Syria, to permanently do away with the Saracens,[136] and to return the Holy Land to the Christians. But the Saracens, learning about Ghazan's coming and realizing that they could not withstand his might, burned everything in the lands through which they would pass, gathering up the crops and animals, so that those who arrived would find neither provision nor food. Learning what the Saracens had done, Ghazan thought to spend that winter by the Euphrates, and to set out at the coming of spring when the grass would start growing. For the Tartars were more concerned about their horses than about themselves, for they themselves eat little.

Then Ghazan summoned the King of Armenia who came and encamped by the river. The multitude of soldiers was so great that it extended along the length of the river, two days'[137] journey, from Fort Kak'aw[138] to Fort Labir,[139] which had surrendered to Ghazan before the attack. While they remained there waiting for the [right] season and weather to deliver the Holy Land from the Saracen's control, it was related to Ghazan that the aforementioned Baidu once again had invaded Ghazan's land and done much damage and had driven out the men [Ghazan] had left there to hold the land. Therefore, Ghazan returned to his place, planning to enter the realm of Syria the next year. Ghazan was sorely displeased that the matter of the Holy Land had been delayed so long.

---

136 O.E. text: *"Sultan of Egypt"*.
137 O.E. text: *"three days"*.
138 *Kak'aw*: Rakka.
139 *Labir*: Bira.

He ordered Qutlugh-Shah to enter the realm of Syria with 40,000 Tartars and take the city of Damascus, putting to the sword as many as he could. He also ordered the King of Armenia to go with his men along with Qutlugh-Shah's 40,000 into the realm of Syria laying waste to everything. They had expected to find the Sultan in that country, as in the past, but he was not there. They heard that he was at Gaza and would not leave there. And so, they came to the city of Homs, besieged it, took it, and killed all the Saracens [and put all the men and women to the sword without any mercy. They found there great riches and plenty of livestock and provisions.

Then they came to Damascus and besieged it. Now the citizens sent messengers requesting three days grace, after which they would surrender, and this request was granted. The Tartars who went on ahead captured some of the Saracens and sent them to Qutlugh-Shah who received them humanely. He learned from them that some two days distant there were 12,000 Saracens who were expecting the Sultan's arrival any day. Qutlugh-Shah went there to capture them unawares. But when he reached the place, he heard that the Sultan and his men had arrived. When Qutlugh-Shah and the King of Armenia realized that the Sultan had arrived, they planned what to do. Because it was almost evening, they planned to rest and the next day to prudently go against the Sultan. However, Qutlugh-Shah, who despised the Sultan, did not want to delay, but instead to face the enemy right away. But those [Saracens] who were near the lake released the waters, creating a stream of water that the Tartars had great difficulty crossing. After Qutlugh-Shah, the King of Armenia and most of their troops, had crossed, they valiantly set upon their enemy, killing all they encountered and pursuing them until night. The Sultan did not attack them but remained by the mountain and lake. That night Qutlugh-Shah camped with his men by a mountain, except for 10,000 troops who were unable to cross the water by daylight. The next day Qutlugh-Shah deployed his men to fight, but the Sultan, did not budge the second day either, for he was in a safe place for defending himself and his troops. The Tartars took great pains to get the Saracens out of that place, but they could not effect this. The battle lasted from morning until noon, but because there was a shortage of drinking water [the Tartars] were tormented with exhaustion and thirst. So they went back to find water, one after another, until they came to the plain of Damascus where they found pasture and water enough. Qutlugh-Shah ordered a rest for his men and horses so that they would be refreshed to return and fight against the Sultan.

Now the Damascenes that night aimed the waters of the river into that plain, throwing all [the Tartars] into panicked confusion, and causing the loss of many horses, pack animals and weapons. At dawn they escaped the danger of the waters, but not without having lost many soldiers. Because their bows and arrows were rendered useless by the inundation of water, [the Tartars] could have been defeated easily with almost no survivors, had the enemy attacked them at that point.

The Tartars turned back because of the loss of their horses and in eight days reached the Euphrates River. But since the water-level had risen, they were obliged to cross on horseback as best they could. Many Tartars, Armenians and Georgians[140] were drowned. And so the Tartars returned to their confusion, not because of the power of their enemy, but because of bad planning; for Qutlugh-Shah might have avoided all that hardship if he had followed good counsel. I, brother Het'um, the narrator of this episode, was present there. If I have spoken overly long about this matter, please pardon me. I have done so to highlight similar dangers, since matters which are planned out properly should end successfully.

After the King of Armenia had crossed the Euphrates, not without great effort and loss of men, he went to see Ghazan in the city of Nineveh about returning to Armenia. Ghazan received him with honor, requiting him for the harm suffered with 1,000 Tartars, and designating a quantity of money for them from the King of the Turks. The King of Armenia returned to his land with them, encouraged by Ghazan to keep his country well until they would be able to cross to the Holy Land.

---

140   O.E. text: *"many Georgians and Tartars"*.

CHAPTER 45

HOW THE SULTAN MADE A TRUCE WITH THE KING OF ARMENIA

The King of Armenia returned to his country, but afterwards he had little rest. For that same year, almost monthly, the Sultan sent a great number of warriors who ruined practically all the lands of Armenia and wasted all the plains; as a result, the realm of Armenia was in worse condition than ever before. But omnipotent, all-merciful God took pity on the Christians. In the month of July, 7,000 Saracens, the best of the Sultan of Egypt's house, entered the country of Armenia, wasting everything up to the city of Tarsus, site of the nativity of the Apostle Paul. After committing many wicked deeds, they turned back. But the King of Armenia and his troops arose before them and, with help from On High, battled with them near the city of Ayas, either capturing or putting to the sword all but three hundred men, who escaped. This transpired on Sunday, July 18th. After this beating, the Saracens thereafter did not dare return to Armenia. And the Sultan of Egypt made and held to a peace treaty and armistice with the King of Armenia.

CHAPTER 46

REGARDING THE DIVISION OF MY BOOK FROM THE BEGINNING

I, brother Het'um, was a participant in the aforementioned [events] and had long since decided to become a cleric. But because of difficult circumstances in the Armenian kingdom, I was unable to abandon my lords and friends in such perilous straits and depart to fulfill my personal desires. However, through Providence from On High the desire and hope of my heart was realized. I went to Cyprus and entered the Praemonstratensian Order in the year 1305. Thank God that the kingdom of Armenia is in good condition; and through the strengthening of God may it regain its former status by the efforts of Lewon, who sparkles with every virtue.

I, who wrote this book, know all that is in the third part in three ways. Events which transpired from the time of Chingiz-Khan, first Emperor of the Tartars, to Monge-Khan, the fourth Emperor, were taken from the histories of the Tartars. [Events] from Monge-Khan to the death of Hulegu, [I] heard from my honorable uncle, King Het'um of Armenia, who was present at all of them. With great diligence [he] retold [it] to his sons and nephews, and had us put [it] in writing for a remembrance. From the beginning of the reign of Abagha-Khan, son of Hulegu, to the third part of the book where the history of the Tartars ends, I speak as one who was present in person; and what I have seen I have recorded accurately.

We have spoken about the deeds and history of the Tartars. Now let us describe their power.

CHAPTER 47

T'AMAR-KHAN, SIXTH RULER OF THE TARTARS, HIS AUTHORITY AND LORDSHIP OVER SUBJECTS

The sixth Great Khan, T'amar-Khan, resides in the great city of Cathay called Eons,[141] built by his father. [The might of this Emperor is great, for he himself could effect more than all the other Tartar princes. His men are more noble, richer and better provisioned in all things than others; for there are great riches in the land of Cathay. There are three kings, rulers of large lordships, who obey this emperor, everything being referred to him and resolved by him. They are: Chapar,[142] Totay,[143] and Tarbanda.[144]

The first king subject to Tamar-Khan, Shap'ar [Chapar], resides in Turkestan, which is closer to the Emperor's lands than are the others. He has under him some 400,000 armed horsemen with good provisions and horses. They are bold and valiant warriors. Sometimes the Emperor wages war with Chapar and would take his lands from him, but he defends them bravely. The lordship of Chapar is all under one lord, though his brother Toqta holds a large part of his land.

The second king, Toqta, dwells in the city of Saray in the realm of Komania. He is able to muster 600,000 warriors[145] possessing better horses and gear than Chapar, but his men are not as brave. Sometimes they war against the King,[146] sometimes against the King of the Hungarians, and sometimes they fight amongst themselves. Currently this king is at peace.

The third king, Gharband, resides in the city of Tabriz in Greater Asia. Under him are 300,000 men of diverse nationalities, all to be respected [as soldiers] who have everything

---

141 *Eons*: Beijing.
142 *Chapar*: Khan of Chagatai (1300-8).
143 *Totay*: Toqta Khan, ruler of Qipchaq (1291-1312).
144 *Tarbanda*: Muhammed Uljeitu Gharbanda or Khar-Banda, Ilkhan of Persia (1304-16).
145 O.E. text: 700,000.
146 *King* Gharabanda.

they need. Now Chap'ar and Toqta had planned to do away with [Gharbanda's] rule, but were unable even though they are stronger in men and lands.

The reason for this is that there are but three roads leading into the realm of Greater Asia. One goes from Turkestan requiring passage of many days through the desert, and no fodder for the horses is to be found there at all. The second route is via Lotorpent[147] and is by the sea. Alexander [the Great] built a city here named the Iron Gate. [This route] is negotiable only in wintertime, but there are trenches and fortresses and armed guards there in the winter. In fact, during that season Toqta's people did attempt to pass along this route secretly. However, in that plain lovely blue birds called seyserach were feeding, and they flew away from the invaders, passed over to the sentries, and warned of the enemy's approach. Therefore, they were ready for them. The third route passes through the great [Black] sea, which the enemy has never attempted to traverse, for the kingdom of Abkhazia is fortified by many people whom one cannot be sure of defeating. In this manner, Gharbanda and his ancestors have defended their lands from the great might of their enemies and neighbors.

---

147 *Lotorpent:* Derbent.

CHAPTER 48

MORE ON THE TARTARS' RELIGION AND CUSTOMS

The Tartars are very diverse in manners and customs, and so it is not possible to describe all of them. They recognize one immortal God on Whom they call for help, but they have no worship of God, neither prayers nor fasts. They regard murder and prostitution as sins. They take many wives and it is obligatory for the son to marry his [widowed] mother, and for the brother, his brother's wife. They regard not removing the bit from a pasturing horse's mouth as a crime punishable by death. The Tartars are brave warriors and soldiers, more obedient to their lords than any other nation. When the lord of the Tartars goes off to war, he gives his soldiers no stipend, but they live off the booty and spoils and give a share of it to their lord. When the Tartars go on an expedition where they expect to find no provisions, they bring with them large quantities of animals, cattle and mares, and live on milk and horsemeat which they greatly esteem. They are skilled in horsemanship and are brave mounted archers, but they are not very good as infantry, as they are slow on foot.

The Tartars are keen in taking cities and fortresses during battle. They do not consider it shameful to turn to flight, if flight is advantageous. Nor are they always so eager to make an attack; instead, if possible, they attack an enemy when the enemy is unable to resist them. Because they are brave warriors, it is difficult to fight with them or to reduce them by pursuit, for they fall back in a set fashion, turning around [in their saddles] and shooting their arrows. When the Tartars are overcome, they flee all together, as close to each other as possible. The Tartars give what they have to people who come to them, and they themselves demand the same from others, taking by force what is not given. They know how to take another's land, but not how to hold it. They are humble when weak, but when strong or in multitudes, they are haughty. They do not want others to lie, but they themselves lie at will, except in military affairs and in confessing wrong-doings, when they will faithfully confess everything, even if they should be condemned or lose their lives.

CHAPTER 49

THE PREREQUISITES FOR STARTING A BATTLE

The following four preconditions are required to start a war: first, the cause must be just; second, the necessities must be on hand for beginning and ending war; third, the enemy's condition and strength must be understood; fourth, the battle must be commenced at a proper time. I, Brother Het'um, having been commanded by Our Lord the Apostle [the Pope] must address this matter. Christians wanting to capture the Holy Land have a just cause, for it is the inheritance of Christ, and our ancestors were forced to bear much from the Saracens. The Christians have sufficient strength, if they would only enter the battle united. I say that no one ought to be in doubt about the second point, for the holy Church of Rome, which is lady and mistress of the entire world, has the power by the grace of God, and with the aid of the good knights and princes of the Christian faith and the servants of Christ, to deliver the Sepulcher and the Holy Lands from the Saracens' power. They hold and occupy these lands because of our sins. I will speak at greater length on the third and fourth points for a good surgeon ought to know the sickness he is going to treat, just as a king or prince ought to find out about the intent, condition and status of his enemies so that he may start his war wisely, maintain it, and bring it to a good end.

To a prince making war, his enemy's secrets should not be hidden. Things learned in advance can do no harm, though unforeseen matters sometimes trouble many courageous warriors who, while fighting, have no time or room to learn of approaching men and dangers. In all other sorts of endeavors if there is some flaw, a remedy may be found—but not in warfare. For soon after the pain follows the cost. Consequently, to make our narration clearer, we shall speak of the passage to the Holy Land, and also say some things about the status and condition of the lands of Egypt, the forces at Babylon [in Egypt], and their strength.

CHAPTER 50

AFFAIRS OF THE KINGDOM OF EGYPT AND THE SULTAN'S CAPABILITIES

The Sultan of Egypt and Syria, named Melomasur,[148] is a Koman by nationality. His army is composed of various peoples of different nationalities, since the local people there are very feeble in battle. They have few infantry, but many horsemen. Truly the greater part of them are slaves that have been bought and sold, which evil Christian men brought there to sell for greed of money; and others are war-captives who were forced to forsake the Christian religion. The slaves which are purchased are more praised and honored, and it frequently happened that large numbers would be purchased because they would be more loyal to their lord and master. The Sultan of Egypt is always wary and suspicious that disturbances do not break out among his subjects and that he not get killed, for they greatly covet the lordship. Many sultans have been slain in this manner. The forces of Egypt consist of 20,000 cavalry and some of them are good, seasoned fighters, but most are not. They possess choice horses and keen, but not very resistant, mules. But they all require great caring for. The troops in Egypt are always in readiness to serve the Sultan, for all of them reside in Cairo.

The condition of the army in Egypt is such that every man of arms receives wages which do not exceed 120 florins. Each one must have three horses and a camel, to carry their things. When the Sultan brings his men out of the realm of Egypt, he gives them somewhat more, if it pleases him. The Sultan leaves his wages and offices in keeping to his barons, called admirals. To some he gives a hundred [knights]; to some two hundred, more or less, if he wants to honor one more than another. If the Sultan gives power to one admiral to keep a hundred or two hundred knights, he gives him the entire sum for their upkeep.

As a result, there is a great deficiency in his service, because the admirals that provide one or two hundred knights [are providing them as] slaves purchased with their own funds,

---

148 *Melomasur*: Malik al-Mansur Husam-ad-Din Lajin, (1296-98).

delivered with horse and harness and pressed into service. After [the admirals] give them horses and gear and receive wages for them, all the remainder [of the Sultan's funds] go into their own pockets. And so, there are few valiant men among them.

CHAPTER 51

THE AUTHORITY OF THE SULTAN IN THE LAND OF SYRIA

In the country of Syria are 5,000 troops who live off the rents of the land. There are, moreover, foreigners: Bedouins and Torkuats'ik'[149] who know well how to take cities. They are of great help to the Sultan when he wants to besiege some land, for he may have them without giving them any wages, just some [booty]. But as for going into battle or defending his land, the above-mentioned Bedouins and Turkmens would do nothing for the Sultan without huge payments. If the Sultan would try to force them, they would leave—the Turkmens going into the mountains, and the Bedouins to the deserts of Arabia. But the Sultan has a sergeant in the country of Moyllebech[150] and around Mount Lebanon and in the land of the Assassins who might help him in besieging a city or a castle to hold their own land. But they would not leave their country for the Sultan, nor can he force them, for there are great mountains there. The Sultan of Egypt is very skilled in taking cities and castles, and they set upon the land in diverse manner: for by crossbows, stones, tunneling under the ground, fire that cannot be extinguished and other means, they can easily take a land without any peril.

---

149 *Torkuats'ik'*: Turkmens.
150 *Moyllebech*: Baalbek.

CHAPTER 52

THE KINGDOM OF EGYPT AND HOW IT CHANGED HANDS

The Greeks [Byzantines] held the lordship of Egypt through generals and administrators who collected the taxes and sent them to the Emperor. They ruled until the year 704. The Egyptians, however, not wanting to endure such a burden, surrendered to the Saracens. And they chose their lord from the clan of Muhammad and called him Caliph. And all their lords have been called caliphs. They held that lordship for 347 years. Then those Medians called Kurds occupied the lordship of Egypt.

Now in 1053 A. D. the King of Jerusalem, Amarikos,[151] assembled as many Christian troops as possible, and entered the country of Egypt, conquering many cities and villages as is written in the book of the conquests of the Holy Land. When the Caliph saw that he could not resist the Christians, he sent to the Sultan of Aleppo, called Xarakon,[152] who came with a great host of soldiers and caused the Christians to flee. Seeing the greatness of Egypt, he had the Caliph arrested and thrown into jail. And he himself, a Khwarezmian from the country of Media, became the Sultan and lord of Egypt. He was the first of his nationality to be lord of Egypt.

After his death, his son, Saladin succeeded, a man who conquered the Christians and took Jerusalem. This Saladin was so successful that he defeated the King of Jerusalem, and took his cities by force, and took various other lands of the Christians, as it states in the book of the conquests of the Holy Land. He was succeeded by his brothers and nephews down to the time of Sultan Melik'sala,[153] who reigned when the Tartars subjugated the kingdom of Komania and were selling many Komans. He sent a large sum of money to purchase Komans, especially the young ones, who were then brought to Egypt. He loved them dearly, had them nourished and trained to ride, shoot

---

151 *Amarikos:* Amalric I.
152 *Xarakon*: Asad-ad-Din al-Mansur Shirkuh.
153 *Melik'sala*: al-Malik as-Salih Aiyyub Najm-ad-Din, sultan (1240-49).

arrows and bear other arms, and he always kept them around him.

It was in this period when the venerable Louis,[154] King of France, had crossed the sea and been captured by the Saracens, that the Komans killed the Sultan and set up a Koman by the name of Turkinia.[155] Therefore, the King of France and his brother were the sooner ransomed and released from jail. In this manner the Komans began to hold the lordship in Egypt. The Komans of Egypt are called Qipchaqs in the Orient. Now after a few days, Kat'oz, also a Koman, put Turkinia to the sword and himself became Sultan under the name of Melikmees.[156] He was the one who defeated the Tartar general Kit-Bugha whom Hulegu had sent to defend the land of Syria. When Melikmees returned to Egypt the Koman Bntuxtar killed him on the road. Bntuxtar, who styled himself Melik dayir,[157] was an extremely shrewd man. He captured numerous places, and the city of Antioch in the year 1268. And he caused many losses to the King of Armenia.

During the reign of this Sultan, the King of England[158] waged war. The Sultan planned to kill him through a murderous Assassin who stabbed him with a poisoned sword. But after enduring numerous agonies, Edward recovered. After this, Melik dayir was poisoned to death in Damascus and his son, Melik'sayit, became Sultan.[159] But the Koman Elshi[160] soon chased him out of the kingdom of Egypt and himself became Sultan. He captured the city of Tripoli in the year 1289.

---

154 *Louis VI,* Saint Louis, crusading 1249-54.
155 *Turkinia:* al-Malik al-Nu'izz Izz-ad-Din Aybak (sultan 1250-57).
156 *Melikmees:* al-Muzaffar Saif-ad-Din Kutuz (sultan 1259-60).
157 *Melik dayir:* Baibars (1260-77).
158 *King of England:* Edward I, crusading 1271-72, while prince of Wales.
159 *Melik'sayit:* al-Malik as Said Nasir-ad-din Muhammad (sultan 1277-79).
160 *Koman Elshi:* al-Mansur Saif-ad-Din Kalwun al-Elfy (sultan 1279-90).

CHAPTER 53

HOW THE CITY OF ACRE WAS TAKEN FROM THE CHRISTIANS

The next year Elfy wanted to besiege the city of Acre, but he was poisoned by his general. But the latter, too, was cut to pieces by others. Then Elfy's son, Melataperah, was made Sultan.[161] He took the city of Acre in the year 1291. But on one occasion when he went to the privy, he was slain by his servant who wanted to become Sultan. Then that man himself was slain by others.

After this they set up as lord and Sultan Meliknazir,[162] the brother of Malik al-Ashraf. He is the one currently ruling. Because he was very young, he was given the Tartar Kit-Bugha as a guardian, a servant bought from his father. He ravished the lordship and had the young Sultan put in Fort Montreal, providing him with all the necessities. Kit-Bugha had himself called Melik'hatel.[163] Under him there was such a short supply of victuals that all the Saracens would have died had not the Christians, through love of gain, increased the food supply.

When the Tartars came, the Sultan assembled his troops and went to defend the country of Syria. And he loved his [Tartar] people dearly. Therefore, in envy, the Komans took the lordship from him and set up as lord Lashim.[164]

This Lajin would not kill Kit-Bugha because he was his friend, but instead he gave him a country called Sarta.[165] Then he gave him the lordship of Hamah, but he would not allow Kit-Bugha to live in Egypt. Lajin remained in the castle of Cairo

---

161 *Melataperah*: Malik al-Ashraf Salah-ad-Din Khalil (1290-93).
162 *Meliknazir*: al-Malik al-Nasir Muhammad (1293-94, 1299-1309, 1310-41).
163 *Melik'hatel*: Malik al-Adil Ketboge, 1294-96.
164 *Lashim*: Malik al-Mansur Husam-ad-Din Lajin (sultan 1296-98).
165 *Sarta*: Sarkhad (near Damascus).

for three years out of fear of his men. On one occasion, when he descended for sport into the plain, his horse fell with him and crushed his leg. Another time, during a game of chess, his servant snatched the Sultan's knife and stabbed him in the head. The murderer was beheaded there. Then great discord arose among the Saracens until they placed the young Sultan Meliknazir on the throne. He is the one that Kit-Bugha had left in the Krak of Mount Royall. He is the one who defeated Ghazan in battle, and he is currently ruling.

Please forgive me for dwelling on the buying and selling of Komans and the sultans who were of their lineage. I do this to demonstrate that the Saracens would not last long if an adversity befell them which prevented [the Komans] from exiting Egypt and going into another land with troops.

CHAPTER 54

THE POSITION AND CIRCUMSTANCES OF EGYPT

The kingdom of Egypt is extremely large and well-situated. In length it is a journey of fifteen days; in breadth, only of three. And it is like an island surrounded by desert and sand. On one border is the Greek Sea;[166] on the east it borders the kingdom of Syria, but with an eight days' journey through sand. On the west is the Barbary land called Bardad,[167] but between the two stretches a fifteen days' journey through desert. On the south is a king of black Christians, with an intervening twelve days' journey through desert.

In the kingdom of Egypt are five districts: first and largest is Sayit; second, Demesor; third, Alexandria; fourth, Rheshint, an island surrounded by rivers; and fifth, Timiad.[168] Cairo is the greatest city, large and very wealthy. Nearby is an old city called Msr, by the Nile River, which is known as the Gehon in Scripture, and which irrigates and fertilizes the entire country. This river has an abundance of fish and is navigable. There are also crocodiles in the river which devour men, fish, and other animals. The river begins to swell during the month of August, until the feast of St. Michael, and it waters the country for forty days, after which it begins to weaken. In the city of Msr is a marble column which measures the water's level, and the price of things depends on the abundance of water. The river water is potable, but since it is too hot to drink directly, they first cool it in earthen vessels.

---

166 *Greek Sea*: Mediterranean Sea.
167 *Barbary*: North African; *Bardad*: Libya.
168 *Sayit* (Said), *Demesor* (Misr), *Rheshint* (Rashid [Rosetta]) and *Timiad* (Damietta).

In the kingdom of Egypt there are two harbors on the ocean, Alexandria and Damietta. Alexandria is well fortified. The citizens drink water from the Nile River brought by underground tunnels into cisterns. Damietta, also by the Nile River, is surrounded by walls. It was captured twice by Christian forces: once by the King of Jerusalem and other Christian troops from the East, and a second time by the blessed Louis, King of France. The city was given back to the Saracens in exchange for the King's liberty. It was totally pulled down and rebuilt far from the river and the sea. This place was named New Damietta. The old Damietta is all devastated. The Sultan receives many goods via the ports of Alexandria and Damietta. They have [for food] the flesh of domesticated birds, kids, fowl, but few cattle, for which they substitute camel meat.

There are some Christians dwelling in the realm of Egypt called Copts, who observe the Jacobite rite and have many monasteries which they hold freely and in peace. These Copts are the oldest heirs of the land of Egypt, for the Saracens began ruling after them. There are things that are not found in Egypt which the Egyptians could not get without the help of others—such as iron and other things. Because of this, they could not long endure if deprived of them. In the entire realm of Egypt there is no walled fortress excepting the city of Alexandria, which is well walled. The Sultan resides in the fortress of Cairo, which is not strong. The entire land of Egypt is defended by knights. Thus, if the troops of Egypt were overcome, the land could be quickly conquered without any danger.

BOOK FOUR

WHEN IS THE TIME TO START THE WAR?

Briefly let me reprise this sentiment:

> *"Ecce nunc tempus acceptabile,*
> *ecce nunc dies salutis."*[169]

For truly the time is appropriate and right to commence war against the enemies of the holy faith. Now is the right time to give help to the Holy Land which has been in the hands of believers in evil for a long time. Now is the right time for the lovers of Christ to consider going to the Holy Land so that the Holy Sepulcher of Our Lord may be delivered from the enemies' hands—that is the beginning of our faith. Nor in times past can we recall such an apt time as now exists, as God by His pity and mercy has shown us in diverse ways. For first, God Almighty, full of mercy, has given us a pastor and Holy Father who is truly a Christian and full of virtue and who, since being seated on the Apostolic Throne has both night and day thought how he might help the Holy Land free itself from the hands of the enemies of the holy faith (who have harmed the name of Christ and the Holy Sepulcher of Our Lord). So that [the people] may truly believe that God has turned His merciful eyes to behold the Holy Land, [He] has given [us] a redeemer on earth (it is the Apostolic Father [Pope]) during whose tenure by the mercy of God, the Holy Land of Jerusalem which has been kept under the servitude of our enemies because of our sins, shall be delivered to the control of Christian men.

---

169 *"Behold, now is the acceptable time; behold, now the day of salvation"* (II Corinthians 6:2).

WHY THEY SHOULD GO INTO THE HOLY LAND

God has shown us clearly that the time is now right for the Holy Land to be delivered out of the enemy's control. For by the grace of God, the kings and princes of Christian lands are currently in a good state and there is peace among them and [they] no longer engage in warfare and arguments as they were wont to do in the past. Consequently, it is likely that God Almighty will deliver the Holy Land. All Christian men of different lands and realms should be clothed in faith and devotion to take up the Cross and cross over the sea to aid the Holy Land and to give their bodies and wealth for the honor and reverence of Our Lord Jesus Christ, valiantly and with good will.

HOW THE ENEMIES OF THE CHRISTIAN FAITH WERE REDUCED AND PUT DOWN

Now is the proper time since God demonstrated to the Christian people that the power of the enemies of the Christian faith has diminished; also by warfare with the Tartars who defeated them, they lost countless men in battle; also that the Sultan reigning in Egypt is an evil and worthless man. Moreover, by the power of the Tartars, all the Saracen princes who were accustomed to aid the Sultan are dead. Only one of them, the Sultan of Mardin, is left, and he has lately submitted to the Tartars. Therefore, at this time, the Holy Land could be recovered and the realm of Egypt and Syria conquered without any danger or pain. And also, the power of the enemies might be brought down more easily at present than in times past.

HOW GHARBANDA, KING OF THE TARTARS, OFFERED TO GO TO THE HOLY LAND WITH HIS FORCES

God has also shown the Christians that the time is right because the Tartars themselves have offered to give help to the Christians against the Saracens. For this reason, Gharbanda, King of the Tartars, sent his messengers offering to use all his power to undo the enemies of the Christian land. Thus, at present, the Holy Land might be recovered with the help of the Tartars and the realm of Egypt, easily conquered without peril or danger. And so Christian forces ought to leave for the Holy Land without any delay, for there is great danger in putting it off: the danger that Gharbanda, who is now a friend, should fail, and another [khan] might arise who would practice Muhammad's ways and agree with the Saracens, events which might lead to great damage and peril for the Christian lands and for the Holy Land across the sea.

Before Your Reverence, Holy Father,[170] I confess that I am not sufficiently learned to give counsel concerning so great a matter as the passage over the sea to the Holy Land. Yet, so that I do not incur the punishment of the disobedient son, I will obey the command of Your Holiness, which no good Christian should refuse. So, I shall give advice according to my limited knowledge, as wise men advise, first requesting pardon for whatever I say.

---

170 *Holy Father:* Pope Clement V, 1305-14

CONCERNING THE ENEMY'S STRENGTHS AND WEAKNESSES

For the honor of Our Lord Jesus Christ, I hope to accomplish my task. I say that for the Holy Land to be conquered with the least pain and trouble, it is appropriate that Christian forces enter the land and set upon their enemies when the latter are troubled by some misfortune. For if the Christians were to undertake this enterprise when their enemies are in good shape, they could not accomplish their endeavor without great danger and suffering. Let us discuss precisely what constitutes advantage and what disadvantage. Affairs are advantageous for the enemy when the Saracens have a wise and valiant Sultan and lord who can hold his lordship without fear of rebellion. Another advantage for the enemy may be when they have been at peace and without any war with the Tartars or others for a long period, and when they have great abundance of corn and other goods in the realm of Syria; and when the routes are secure and open by land and sea so that the things which the enemy needs may be brought to them from foreign countries without any trouble; when the Saracens are at peace with the Nubians and with the Bedouins of the Egyptian desert so that they make no war or quarrel; and when the Turkmens and Bedouins dwelling in the realm of Egypt and Syria obey the Sultan of Egypt. With the conditions just mentioned, the enemies' power could rise so much that it would be impossible to overcome them.

THE NAMES OF THE NINE SULTANS WHO WERE SLAIN AND POISONED

On the other hand, adversity might befall the enemy in various forms: when they rise up and kill their Sultan or lord as they have done in times past, and often do. For since the kinfolk of the Komans [Qipchaq] began to hold the lordship in Egypt, nine men have been designated sultans and lords over them. And of these nine sultans that have been in Egypt, the following are known to have been killed by the sword: Turquenie;[171]; Chocas,[172] Lachyn;[173] two others were poisoned: Bedocdar[174] and Elsy.[175] Two others were sent into exile: Melecuaser[176] and Gynboga.[177] Furthermore, this Melecuaser, who is the current Sultan, was once put out of his office and lordship and [the events of] his life point to an evil end.

---

171 *Turquenie:* al-Malik al-Mu'izz Izz-ad-Din Aybak, 1250-54.
172 *Chocas:* al-Muzaffar Saif-ad-Din Kutuz, 1259-60.
173 *Lachyn:* Malik al-Mansur Husam-ad-Din Lajin, 1296-98.
174 *Bedocdar:* al-Malik Rukn-ad-Din Bibars Bunduqdar (Baibars) 1260-77.
175 *Elsy:* al-Mansur Saif-ad-Din Kalawun al-Elfy, 1279-90.
176 *Melecuaser:* al-Malik al Nasir Mohamed, 1293-94, 1299-1309, 1310-41.
177 *Gynboga:* Malik al-Adil Ketboge, 1294-96.

PROVISION AGAINST THE SULTAN OF EGYPT

The enemy might experience adversity when the Nile River rises but does not water the ground as much as is necessary [for agriculture]. Then the Saracens of Egypt would be in great need and hunger. It is not so long ago that these conditions obtained and they would have died of hunger had it not been for Christians who, out of greed for money, brought them provisions. When such need should befall the enemy, they would become impoverished and forced to sell their horses and reduce their forces; and thus, they would be unable to leave Egypt and enter Syria. Each [soldier] must carry with him all such things and baggage as he would need for eight days—for himself, his animals and household. For they encounter only sand and dunes during this eight-day journey. Consequently, whoever lacks horses and camels would not have the power to depart from Egypt, and thus the Sultan would be troubled that he could not come to aid the realm of Syria. Furthermore, it would be a great adversity to the enemy, having warred a long time, if the sea routes were kept such that the things that they need most such as iron and steel could not be brought into their country from other countries. Without such things they could not long endure. Moreover, if the Nubians or Bedouins commenced war against the Sultan, he might be so bothered by it that he could not leave Egypt and go to Syria. [Another opportunity] would be if the land of Syria is in need and has had a bad season due to dryness or Tartar warfare. Should the sea routes fail, the host of Egypt could not come to stay in Syria, since they would be unable to bring anything to Syria out of Egypt or other counties and could not even leave Egypt. So, if the enemies experience some of these adversities, without fail they could not leave Egypt or go to Syria. Then the Christians might occupy the realm of Jerusalem, might repair the cities and castles and fortify them in such a way that they would never fear the power of their enemies.

HOW AMBASSADORS SHOULD BE SENT TO GHARBANDA, A KING OF THE TARTARS, SO THAT THE ENEMIES SHOULD HAVE NOTHING BROUGHT TO THEM

As we have already discussed the fortunes and misfortunes which might befall the enemies, we shall describe in this part the beginning of the passage [expedition] to the Holy Land. I think for the safety and profit of the passage that at the outset a certain number of horsemen and footmen should go there to get familiar with the enemies' strength. It seems to me that these numbers should be sufficient at present: a thousand knights, ten galleys and three thousand workers. In addition, a legate should be sent by the Church and a wise and valiant captain to voyage with them to the island of Cyprus in the realm of Armenia, as they think best. After that, without any delay, with the counsel of the King of Armenia, they should send messengers to Gharbanda, a king of the Tartars, requiring two things. One that Gharbanda assure that nothing should get to the enemies via his territories. The other [requirement] is that he should send his messengers and men to make war in the countries of Meletur[178] and ruin and waste the Aleppo area. After that, we pilgrims and those [forces] from the realm of Cyprus and Armenia should make war and bravely invade the enemies' lands by sea and by land. They should take pains that nothing enter the enemies' lands by sea. Also, our Christian forces might fortify the isle of Corcose[179] which is well situated to intercept the galleys and do great damage to our enemies. Now I shall leave off describing the beginning of the war and turn to [a description] of the enemies themselves since knowledge of their condition and state must guide the counsel of the wise men implementing the present matter. The profits and benefits that might come from this first voyage and passage I shall now briefly mention.

---

178 *Meletur:* Melitene (Malatya).
179 *Corcose:* Ruad.

HOW THE SULTAN OF EGYPT SHOULD BE MADE SUBJECT TO THE CHRISTIANS AND THE TARTARS

The first consideration is this: the first passage should be arranged in such a manner that the enemies become so sorely troubled by the actions of the other Christian forces in those parts of the east, and by the Tartars, that they have no rest, but instead would suffer great worries and losses. For if the Christians and the Tartars waged war against the Sultan of Egypt by sea and by land in the realm of Syria, then the Sultan would be obliged to send his troops to keep and defend the roads, and the cities close to the sea while all others might be assailed. If the Tartars started fighting in the area around Meleton[180] in the land of Aleppo, the Sultan's men would be sent on a twenty-five-day journey [to get there] and they would be coming from Babylon.[181] They would be hurried, would lose their horses and weapons, and would be so weary and troubled that they could not endure. In three or four ways the enemy could lose their belongings and suffer great damages. Further, the enemy might be greatly troubled by the first passage [expedition], for with the arrival of the ten galleys of the passage, with the help of those coming from the realm of Armenia and of Cyprus, the enemies' lands might be completely ruined, and the galleys could return safely to the island of Corcose. Similarly, if the Sultan wanted to keep and defend the lands just mentioned, he would be forced to come in person and bring with him all of his forces from Babylon[182] to Syria, so that he would have enough men to help all the coastline. Leaving the realm of Egypt to go to Syria would be perilous and damaging to the Sultan. He would fear treason from his own men, while the activities of the Christian forces would cause them such trouble that there would be no end to

---

180 *Meleton:* Melitene (Malatya).
181 *Babylon:* Not of Mesopotamia, but Fustat in Egypt (south of Cairo).
182 *Babylon:* Fustat.

the injury. He would consume and waste all his treasure, as it is hard to believe the enormous sums that the Sultan and his men spend and consume every time they leave Egypt for Syria. Using the aforementioned galleys, the sea routes and ports might be held in such a way as to prevent anything getting to the enemy—things they need and cannot long endure without, such as iron and steel and other goods that are brought to them from foreign countries. Moreover, the enemy would lose the taxes from the sea ports, which constitute a great sum of goods and treasure.

Should it happen that the enemies are troubled by some adversity and could not leave Egypt or aid the land of Syria, then the pilgrims of the first passage might well retake the city of Tripoli with the help of other Christian forces of the Orient. Around Mount Lebanon dwell Christian forces, about 40,000 good squires, who would greatly help the pilgrims. They have risen up against the Sultan many times, doing him and his men great harm and damage. Moreover, if Tripoli could be fortified, the Christian forces could hold it until the time of the general passage and might also take all the surrounding country, retaining the Tripoli area. This would make it easy for those coming in the general passage, since if they found a ready port there, they would surely use it.

Should it happen that the Tartars occupied the realm of the Holy Land, the Christian forces of the first passage should be ready to receive the Tartar lands and keep them. I, having a reasonable knowledge of the Tartars' will, quite frankly believe that all the lands [the Tartars] conquer from the Saracens they would willingly give in keeping to the Christian forces. For the Tartars cannot live in that country due to the great summer heat. Consequently, they would be glad that the Christian forces hold and keep them. The Tartars never fight with the Sultan of Egypt for greed of obtaining lands and cities, since they have all of Asia in their subjugation. They fight because the Sultan has always been their principal enemy and has harmed and damaged them more than anyone else, including in warfare with their own neighbors. For the reasons stated above, I believe the following numbers [of troops] will be sufficient: a thousand knights, ten galleys, and 3000 squires. I think that in this initial [expedition] twice as many men would not accomplish as much and the expense and cost would greatly multiply.

Three other benefits might accrue from this first passage. Since the pilgrims of the first passage would have spent a season there and would then know the condition and manner of the land and of the enemy, they could give warning to those other pilgrims arriving in the general passage. Let us take [for example the possible situation with] the Tartars who, because of war or other matters or excuses, would not give help to the Christian forces against the Saracens, and that the Sultan and his men were in prosperity, and that it would not be an easy thing to conquer the Holy Land and deliver it from the enemy's power. You, Holy Father, then knowing the condition of the Holy Land, when considering the general passage would have better advice and counsel about what things would be suitable, whether to send over the general passage or to delay it for a suitable time. And thus all dangers from the enemy could be avoided.

If Your Holiness will permit me, I would make two other suggestions. One is that Your Holiness should write to the King of the Georgians (who are a Christian [people] and perhaps more devoted than any other nation to pilgrimage and the sacred relics of the Holy Land) for them to give help and support to the pilgrims to recover the Holy Land. I truly believe, for the honor of God and for reverence to Your Holiness, that they would fulfill your orders. For they are devout Christians and men of great power, valiant men of arms, and neighbors of the realm of Armenia. Second, Holy Father, You should write to the King of the Nubians (who are Christians and were converted to the Christian faith by Saint Thomas in the holy land of Ethiopia) so that they wage war against the Sultan and his men. I truly believe that these Nubians, for the honor of Our Lord and out of reverence to Your Holiness, would make war against the Sultan and his men and would cause harm and damage to their power, creating great trouble for the Sultan and his men. These letters might be sent to the King of Armenia who would have them translated into their language and send them by your messengers.

In accordance with my limited understanding I have described, devoutly and honestly, what things are necessary for the initial passage to aid the Holy Land. Now, in willing obedience to Your Holy Father's command, I will add to this what is required for the general passage over the sea.

THE GENERAL PASSAGE

The general passage could be undertaken via three routes. One would be via Barbary[183] but I would not advise it, given the condition of the country. Another would be by way of Constantinople, which as is known, is the route taken in the past by Godfrey of Bullyen[184] and other pilgrims. I fully believe that the general passage might easily reach the city of Constantinople. But going through the Braz of Georgie[185] and by the Turks, the way would be uncertain, for Saracen Turkmens dwell in Turkey. Truly the Tartars may deliver and ensure the route and might order that provisions be brought into the land of Turkey at reasonable price, sufficient for the pilgrim host and horses. As everyone knows, the other route is by sea.

Therefore, if the passage will go by sea, at every port ships must be fitted out and other necessities readied to cross over with the pilgrims. Moreover, it should be at a prearranged and appropriate time, so that all the pilgrims are ready to travel in the ships together, so they might land at Cyprus and rest themselves and their horses from the labors of the voyage. After the general passage has arrived in Cyprus and refreshed itself for a certain period, if the pilgrims of the first passage had [managed to] secure the city of Tripoli or another [city] on the coast of Syria, the expedition might be launched from there, making it much easier for them. But if the pilgrims of the first passage were unable to fortify some land in Syria, then it would be necessary for the general passage to go by way of the realm of Armenia. As mentioned, the pilgrims should refresh themselves and their horses in the realm of Cyprus until Michaelmas so that they might safely cross to the realm of Armenia. There they will find whatever they need. Truly they might tarry

---

183 *Barbary:* North Africa.
184 *Godfrey of Bullyen:* Godfrey of Bouillon (d. 1100).
185 *Braz of Georgie:* Bosphorus.

in the city of Tersot[186] more easily because they would find great abundance of water and pasturage for their horses there; and from the realm of Turkey which is close by, they could bring in provisions and horses and whatever they may need; in the land of Armenia, also. They might stay all winter in Armenia. When the pasture is ready, the pilgrim hosts could go to Antioch (a day's journey from the land of Armenia), thence the ships might go by sea to the port of Antioch, and thus the host [traveling on the] sea and the host [traveling on the] land would be close to each other. Next, the pilgrims should occupy the city of Antioch which they would take quickly with God's help, then they could refresh themselves in this land for a certain number of days. They could ruin and ravish their enemies' lands thereabout and thereby learn about their condition, state and will. In this area of Antioch dwell Christians who are good squires, who would come to the Christian forces in good will and perhaps do them good service. When the pilgrims depart from Antioch, they could go by the shore to the city of Lyche.[187] This route would be shorter and better (and the host of Armenia could follow close after the [European] forces by land). Indeed, close to [the castle of] Margat[188] by the sea is a stretch which troubles most people passing it. Should it happen that the enemy has fortified this area in such a way that the pilgrims cannot pass, our men might return to Antioch without any danger. They could [also] go by way of Ephemye[189] toward Cesar [Shaizar] by the banks of the Renell River [Orontes] upward. Going by this route, the host would find good pasture and water and the enemies' lands filled with provisions and other goods, giving them great ease. By this route our men might go to the city of Haman,[190] which is

---

186 *Tersot:* Tarsus.
187 *Lyche:* Latakia.
188 *Margat:* Marqab.
189 *Ephemye:* Apamea.
190 *Haman:* Hama.

a rich city, which the Christian forces might shortly occupy. Should the enemy happen to defend Haman (since it is a rich city), then they could not come to battle against the Christians who would have the advantage fighting in that place and would easily overcome their enemies.

If the Christian forces overcome the Sultan's host, thereafter they would encounter no further obstacles. So they should go straight to the city of Damas [Damascus] which they could take or [the inhabitants] could surrender by treaty. With the Sultan overcome, the [forces of] Damascus would not hold out, but would surrender with good will and live there safely, as they did after Halcon[191] and Casan[192] had beaten the Sultan. If the Christian forces take Damascus, they could easily conquer what remained. Should the enemy lose the battle, the Christian forces could come to Tripoli in four days from Damascus and repair the city anew. The Christian forces of Mt. Lebanon would give great help to the pilgrims in this regard. If the Christian forces can keep the city of Tripoli, then with the aid of God they will conquer the city of Jerusalem.

Accompanying the Christian forces, I think that a certain number, about 20,000, Tartars might greatly ease and benefit the Christian forces going through the countries. Out of fear of the Tartars, the Bedouins and Turkmens would not dare to approach the Christian hosts. The other advantage would be that the Tartars would be arranging for provisions for the Christian forces and would come from distant countries to get money and other things. From the Tartars, [the Christian troops] could seek and learn information about the enemy. [This is because] the Tartars can freely dash into and out of [an area] night or day, very easily. For battling and besting cities, the Tartars might be valuable, for they are very subtle in such things. However, should it happen that Gharbanda or another in his place arrives with men to enter the land

---

191 *Halcon:* Hulegu.
192 *Casan:* Ghazan.

of Egypt, then it would be wise to redeploy and go far from their company. For the Tartars will not do what the Christians want them to, and the Christians might not follow the Tartars' will since [the Tartars] travel quickly on horseback, and the Christians might not [be able to] follow them because of the footmen. Furthermore, when the Tartars know that they are strong and have power, they are very proud and unreasonable and could not go without doing damage to the Christian forces, which the latter might not tolerate. Great shame and ill will might arise between them. However, there is a good solution to this, namely, that the Tartars should go via the Damascus route which they are used to, while the Christian forces should head for Jerusalem. Thus, traveling far from each other, peace and friendship would be preserved between the Tartars and the Christian forces, and the might of the enemy would be confounded by two [armies] rather than one.

I will suggest another matter to Your Holiness, namely, that the plans of the Christian forces be prudently kept. For in the past, they would not keep their counsel, as a consequence of which they experienced many great sorrows while the enemy escaped many great dangers and have taken from the Christian forces the means of accomplishing their will. If news about the general passage cannot be concealed, as they will be traveling through the world, nonetheless, the enemy could inflict no damage or loss from it. For they would not have the aid of any port, and in different ways the Christian forces could conceal their intentions, appearing to do one thing but then doing something else. The fact that the Tartars could not keep their plans concealed has frequently done them great harm. For the Tartars have a custom that in the first month of January they take counsel of all the things that they have to do during that year. Thus, if they plan to make war against the Sultan of Egypt, their plan is known to everyone soon after. The Saracens send word to the Sultan, and based on that [information] the Sultan prepares against them. The Saracens can keep their counsel well, which has often done them good. At present what has been said about the general passage overseas to the Holy Land is sufficient.

After all this, I humbly pray that [Your] Blessed Holiness will receive my written description about the passage to the Holy Land. If I have said more or less than necessary, please forgive me. For I would not have ventured to give advice on such a great matter as the passage to the Holy Land were it not by the command of You, Holy Father, Who, after being seated on the pastoral throne by the command of God, have with all [Your] heart desired, sought and labored for the Holy Land, the rose of the precious blood of Our Lord Jesus Christ, to be delivered from the evildoers. For this reason, all Christian kings and princes have been called upon to give [You] counsel about assisting in the passage to the Holy Land. Our Lord is full of mercy, experience of which shows us that He will deliver the Holy Land out of the hands of the enemy during the reign of You, Holy Father. We all should humbly pray that [God] grant him who reigns [as Pope] a long and good life, *in saecula saeculorum*. Amen.

Here ends the book, Flower of Histories of the East, compiled by the cleric, Brother Haiton of the Praemonstratensian Order, former lord of Corc,[193] cousin germaine of the King of Armenia on the oversea passage to the Holy Land, by the command of our Holy Father the Apostle [Pope] Clement V in the city of Poitiers. I, Nicholas Falcon, first wrote down this book in French, as the aforementioned Brother Haiton dictated it, without notes or exemplars; and from French translated it into Latin for our Holy Father, the Pope, in the year of Our Lord 1307, in the month of August. *Deo gracias.*

---

193 *Corc:* Korykos.

APPENDICES

APPENDIX I

SMBAT SPARAPET'S LETTER TO KING HENRY I OF CYPRUS, ca. 1248[1]

"We understand it to be the fact that it is five years past since the death of the present Khan's father [Ogedei]; but the Tartar barons and soldiers had been so scattered over the face of the earth that it was scarcely possible in the five years to get them together in one place to enthrone the Khan. For some of them were in India, and others in the land of Chata, and others in the land of Caschar and of Tanchat. This last is the land from which came the Three Kings to Bethlehem to worship the Lord Jesus which was born. And know that the power of Christ has been, and is, so great, that the people of that land are Christians; and the whole land of Chata believes in those three Kings. I have myself been in their churches and have seen pictures of Jesus Christ and the Three Kings, one offering gold, the second frankincense, and the third myrrh. And it is through those Three Kings that they believe in Christ, and that the Khan and his people have now become Christians. And they have their churches before his gates where they ring their bells and beat upon pieces of timber... And I tell you that we have found many Christians scattered all over the East, and many fine churches, lofty, ancient, and of good architecture, which have been spoiled by the Turks. Hence the Christians of the land came before the present Khan's

---

1 The letter is addressed to the King and Queen of Cyprus and others at their court, and was written apparently from Samarkand. Translation from Yule, H. (1866). *Cathay and the Way Thither: Being a Collection of Medieval Notices of China*. (Vol. 1). London.

115

APPENDIX I

grandfather; and he received them most honorably, and granted them liberty of worship, and issued orders to forbid their having any just cause of complaint by word or deed. And so the Saracens who used to treat them with contumely have now like treatment in double measure... And let me tell you that those who set up for preachers (among these Christians), in my opinion, deserve to be well chastised. Let me tell you, moreover, that in the land of India, which St. Thomas the Apostle converted, there is a certain Christian king who stood in sore tribulation among the other kings who were Saracens. They used to harass him on every side, until the Tartars reached that country, and he became their liegeman. Then, with his own army and that of the Tartars, he attacked the Saracens; and he made such booty in India that the whole East is full of Indian slaves; I have seen more than 50,000 whom this king took and sent for sale."

CONCERNING THE TRIP OF THE PIOUS KING OF THE ARMENIANS, HET'UM, TO BATU AND MONGKE-KHAN[2]

The devout, Christ-loving king of the Armenians in the Cilicia area had his seat in the city of Sis. Previously he had sent his brother Smbat, who was his general, to Guyuk-Khan with presents and gifts and [Smbat] returned thence with honor and edicts of acceptance. Now when Mongke-Khan ruled, Batu the great "king's father" and general sent to King Het'um so that he would come to see him and Mongke-Khan. [Batu] dwelled in the northern regions with an incalculable multitude [of troops] under him by the shore of the great, fathomless river Et'il[3] which runs into the Caspian Sea. [Het'um] who feared the sultan of Rum whose name was 'Izz al-Din, travelled [through Rum] secretly and in disguise since he feared the Turks who were his neighbors. Now [the Turks] had an inveterate hatred [for Het'um] for allying with the T'at'ars. [Het'um] speedily traversed ['Izz al-Din's] territory in twelve days and arrived at the city of Kars. He visited Baiju *noyin*, the commander of the T'at'ar army in the East, as well as other grandees, and he was honored by them. Then he stayed in the village of Vardenis at the foot of mount Aragats, opposite Aray mountain, in the home of a prince of Armenian nationality named K'urd. [This prince] was a Christian [and lived in the village with] his sons Vach'e and Hasan, and his wife Xorishah. [Xorishah] was of the Mamikonean line, a daughter of Marzban, and sister to Aslan-bek and Grigor. [Het'um] stayed there until goods from his house, useful presents and gifts were

---

2 This is Chapter 58 of Kirakos of Gandzak's *History of the Armenians* (translated by Robert Bedrosian).
3 *Et'il:* Volga.

APPENDIX II

brought to him from his father, the prince of princes Kostand. At this time [Kostand] was old and had left his sons, Lewon and T'oros, as his substitute. His own pious queen [Zapel] already had passed to Christ. Zapel translates to Elisabeth, the "seventh day of God," and her name suited her, for she was at rest in the will of God: benevolent, merciful and a lover of the poor. [Zapel] was the daughter of the great King Lewon, the first to wear the crown [in Cilician Armenia].

As soon as the great Catholicos Kostand learned that [Het'um] had travelled safely and now had stopped in Greater Armenia, he sent to him the great *vardapet* Yakob, a wise and learned man. [The Catholicos] previously had sent this same man to the Byzantine emperor John (who was ruling in Asia and who had grown strong) and to their patriarch to achieve friendship and unity. [Yakob] went there armed with the prudent words of Scripture and, in the Greek council of inquiry, repudiated the Byzantines who accused us of being Eutychians for saying that there is one nature in Christ. [Yakob] rationally demonstrated through Scripture that the two [natures] are united in Christ, completely divine and completely human, two [natures] in ineffable unity, not losing divinity, not confusing the humanity, glorified in one nature working divinely and humanly. Similarly concerning [the hymn] *Surb Astuats*[4] there are words which we say about the Son, according to the witness of the evangelist John. [Yakob] refuted theologically and on the testimony of Scripture other similar slanders which [the Greeks] had regarding our doctrine. He turned their minds toward friendship and unity with our people, and departed from them in honor. Lord Step'anos the bishop came [to Het'um]; *vardapet* Mxit'ar who was at Skewrha where he had travelled from the Eastern areas came as did the priest Barsegh who was

---

4 *Surb Astuats:* "Holy God".

APPENDIX II

an emissary to Batu. With him came the celibate priest T'oros as well as Karapet who was the king's court priest, a man of mild and scholarly manner; and many princes also came. The king took all these men with him to the land of the Aghuans and through the Darband gate (which is the Chora pass) to Batu and his son Sartakh who was a Christian. [Het'um] was honored by them with many privileges. Then they sent him to Mongke-Khan on a long journey on the other side of the Caspian Sea.

Those who departed [from Batu] left on the sixth of the month of Marer,[5] and on the thirteenth of May crossed the Ayex[6] river and came to Or which is midway between Batu and Mongke-Khan. Then crossing the Ert'ich[7] river they entered the Nayiman[8] country. They came to Xaraxeta[9] and crossed into T'at'arstan on the fourth of the month of Horhi, the thirteenth of September on the celebration of the feast of the Cross, and they saw Mongke-Khan seated in venerable glory. [Het'um] gave the Khan gifts and was honored by him according to his dignity. He remained at the urdo for fifty days and [Mongke-Khan] gave him a noteworthy edict that no one dare harass him or his country. He also gave him a document proclaiming freedom for the Church everywhere.

[Het'um] left [Mongke-Khan] on the fiftieth day, on the twenty-third of the month of Sahmi, on November first. In thirty days [the party] reached Ghumsghur. And they came to Perpalex and Peshpalex and to the sandy country where there are naked wild men with hair on their heads only. The women there have very large and long breasts and the people are mute. In that land are found wild horses of black and yellow colors,

---

5 *Mareri:* the tenth month of the year (May) in the Armenian calendar.
6 *Ayex:* Ural.
7 *Ert'ich:* Irtysh.
8 *Nayiman:* Naiman.
9 *Xaraxeta:* Khara-Khita.

APPENDIX II

and mules of white and black colors, larger than horses or asses, as well as wild camels with two humps.

From there they came to Arhlex, to K'ulluk and Enkax, to Chanpalex, Xut'ap'ay and Ankipalex.

They then entered T'urk'astan. Thence to Ekop'ruk, Dinkapalex and P'ulat. They crossed Sut-k'oln and K'atntsov[10] and came to Alualex and Ilanpalex. Then they crossed the Ilan-su river and over a branch of the Taurus mountains to Dalas and came to Hulegu, who was Mongke-Khan's brother, and who had taken the Eastern regions as his portion.

[The party] then turned from a westerly direction northward and reached Xut'uxch'i, Perk'ant', Sughulghan, Urosoghan, K'ayik'ant', Xuzax (K'amots'), to Xndaxoyr and to Sghnax[11] where the Saljuqs are from; [Xarch'ux] begins at the Taurus mountain and goes as far as P'arch'in where it ends.

They traveled from there to Sartakh, the son of Batu, who was travelling to Mongke-Khan. Then [they went] to Sghnax and Sawran (which is extremely large) to Xarach'ux, Ason, Sawri, Ot'rar, Zurhnux, and Dizak and then after thirty days [came] to Samarqand, Sarhip'ul, K'rman and Bukhara. Then they crossed the great Jehun river,[12] and arrived at Mrmen, Saraxs, and Tus which is opposite Khrasan (which is called Rhoghastan). They entered Mazandaran and [travelled] thence to Pstan, then to the land of Iraq which is in the borders of the Assassins. Then [they travelled] to Tamgha and the great city of Ray and to Qazvin to Awahr, to Zangian, to Miana, thence to Tabriz after twelve days. After twenty-six days they crossed the Erasx river to Sisian to the chief of the T'at'ar army, Baiju *noyin*. Now [Baiju] sent [Het'um] to Xocha *noyin*, a man he had left as his substitute as head of the forces. Meanwhile he himself took the

---

10 *K'atnatsov:* "Milk Sea".
11 *Sghnax:* Xarchux mountain.
12 *Jehun river:* Amu-Darya (Oxus).

APPENDIX II

chiefs of the army and went before Mongke-Khan's brother Hulegu, who was coming to the East.

The pious King Het'um came to the home of prince K'urd in Vardenis village where he had left his goods and baggage, and awaited the return of the priest Barsegh whom he had sent to Batu once more to show him the documents and orders of Mongke-Khan so that [Batu] also would write orders of the same sort.

Then there came to Het'um his vardapets: Yakob whom he had left [in Greater Armenia] for church work, and Mxit'ar (who had returned from Batu before [the latter] travelled to Mongke-Khan); and other bishops and vardapets and priests and Christian princes. [Het'um] received them all with affection for he was an agreeable man, wise and literate. He gave gifts as he could and sent them all off happy. He gave priestly garments to adorn the Church, for [Het'um] greatly loved mass and the Church. He received all the Christian peoples and beseeched them to deal with one another affectionately as brothers and members of Christ, as the Lord commanded: "By this you shall be recognized as my pupils, that you love one another."[13]

[King Het'um] told us many marvellous and unknown things about the barbarian peoples, things he had seen and heard about. He said: "There is a land beyond Ghatayik'[14] where women have the forms of natural women, while the men have the forms of dogs. They are mute, large, and hairy. The dogs let no one enter their land and the dogs hunt from which prey they and the women eat. From the comingling of dogs and women, the males are born in the shape of dogs, the females in the shape of women.

---

13 John 13:35.
14 Cathay, China.

APPENDIX II

"There is, too, a sandy island where a type of bone (which is prized) grows like a tree. It is called Dzknatam[15] and when one is cut, another grows in its place, like horns.

"There is, too, a land of many idol-worshippers who worship extremely large clay idols named Shakmonia [Shakiamuni] and say that he is god for 3040 years. Then another thirty-five *duman* years [elapse] (one duman being 10,000) after which [Shakiamuni] is removed from godship. Then there is another one named Madri [Matreya] of whom they also made a clay image of unbelievable size in a beautiful temple.

"An entire people, women and children included, are priests. They are called Toyink', and have their heads and beards shaven. They wear cloaks like Christian [priests] but [fastened] at the breast, not at the shoulder. They are moderate in eating and marriage. [Men] marry at twenty years of age and until age thirty approach their wives three times a week. From age thirty to age forty they approach them three times a month; from forty to fifty, three times a year; and after fifty, not at all."

The wise king related much else about the barbarian peoples which we omit, lest it seem extraneous to anyone.

Eight months after leaving Mongke-Khan, Het'um reached Armenia. This was in 704 A.E.[16]

---

15 *Dzknatam:* "Fish Tooth".
16 For a scholarly commentary on this chapter see Boyle, J. A. (1964). The Journey of Het'um I, King of Little Armenia, to the Court of the Great Khan. *Central Asiatic Journal,* 9, 175-89.

APPENDIX III

RULERS OF MONGOL EMPIRES

HOUSE OF CHINGIZ

[The Great Khans and the Yuan Dynasty of China]

Chingiz-Khan, 1206-1227

Ogedei, 1229-1241

Guyuk, 1246-1248

Mongke, 1251-1258

Qubilai, 1260-1294

Temur, 1294-1307

Qaishan, 1307-1311

Buyantu, 1311-1320

Gegen, 1320-1323

Yesun-Temur, 1323-1328

Toq-Temur, 1328-1329

Qutuqtu, 1329-1332

Irinchinbal, 1332

Toghan-Temur, 1332-1370

HOUSE OF HULEGU

[The Il-Khans of Iran]

Hulegu, 1256-1265

Abaqa, 1265-1281

Teguder, 1281-1284

Arghun, 1284-1291

Geikhatu, 1291-1295

Baidu, 1295

Ghazan, 1295-1304

Oljeitu, 1304-1316

Abu Sa'id, 1316-1335

APPENDIX III

RULERS OF MONGOL EMPIRES

HOUSE OF JOCHI

[The Khans of the Golden Horde, 1237-1357]

Batu, 1237-1256

Sartaq, 1256-1257

Ulaghichi, 1257

Berke, 1257-1266

Mongke-Temur, 1267-1280

Tode-Mongke, 1280-1287

Tole-Buqa, 1287-1291

Toqta, 1291-1312

Oz-Beg, 1313-1341

Tini-Beg, 1341-1342

Jani-Beg, 1342-1357

HOUSE OF CHAGHATAI

[The Chaghatai Khanate, 1227-1338]

Chaghatai, 1227-1242

Qara-Hulegu, 1242-1246

Yesu-Mongke, 1246-1251

Orghina, 1251-1260

Alughu, 1260-1265/66

Mubarak-Shah, 1266

Baraq, 1266-1271

Negubei, 1271

Toqa-Temur, 1272

Du'a, 1282-1307

Konchek, 1308

Taliqu, 1308-1309

Esen-Buqa, 1310-1318

Kebek, 1318-1326

Elchigidei, 1326

Du'a Temur, 1326

Tarmashirin, 1326-1334

Buzan, 1334

Chingshi, 1334-1338

APPENDIX IV

MEDIEVAL RULERS OF ANTIOCH, CYPRUS, JERUSALEM

RULERS OF ANTIOCH

Bohemond I, 1099-1111
Tancred, Regent, 1101-1103, 1104-1112
Roger of Salerno, Regent, 1112-1119
Baudoin (Baldwin) II of Jerusalem, Regent, 1119-1126
Bohemond II, 1126-1130
Constance, 1130-1164
Raymond of Poitiers, 1140-1149
Reynald of Chatillon, 1153-1160
Bohemond III, 1163-1201
Bohemond IV, Count of Tripoli, 1187-1233, 1201-1216, 1219-1233
Raymond-Ruben, 1216-1219
Bohemond V, 1233-1252
Bohemond VI, 1252-1275
Baybars captures Antioch, 1268
Bohemond VII, titular ruler, 1275-1287

HOUSE OF CYPRUS

Guy of Lusignan, 1192-1194
Amalric of Lusignan, 1194-1205
Hugh I, 1205-1218
Henry I, 1218-1253
Hugh II, 1253-1268
Hugh III, 1268-1284
John I, 1284-1285
Henry II, 1285-1306
Amalric of Tyre, 1306-1310
Henry II, 1310-1324
Hugh IV, 1324-1359
Peter I, 1359-1369
Peter II, 1369-1382
James I, 1382-1398
Janus, 1398-1432
John II, 1432-1458
Charlotte, 1458-1464
James II, 1464-1474
James III, 1473-1474
Catherine Coronaro, 1474-1489

APPENDIX IV

MEDIEVAL RULERS OF ANTIOCH, CYPRUS, JERUSALEM

RULERS OF JERUSALEM

Godfrey of Boulogne, 1099-1100

Baudoin (Baldwin) I of Boulogne, 1100-1118

Baudoin II of Le Bourg, 1118-1131

Queen Melisende, Regent 1131-1152

Fulk of Anjou, 1131-1143

Baudoin III, 1143-1163

Second Crusade, 1147-1149

Amalric I, 1163-1174

Baudoin IV, 1174-1185

Queen Sibyl, 1185-1190

Baudoin V, 1185-1186

Guy of Lusignan, 1186-1192

Jerusalem falls to Saladin, 1187

Third Crusade, 1189-1192

Queen Isabela I, 1192-1205

Henry II of Champagne, 1192-1197

Fourth Crusade, 1202-1204

Queen Maria of Montferrat, 1205-1210

John of Brienne, 1210-1225

Queen Yolanda/Isabella II, 1210-1228

Frederick II Hohenstaufen, 1225-1228

Fifth Crusade, 1228-1229

Ayyubids cede Jerusalem, 1229

Conrad IV Hohenstaufen, 1228-1254

Conrad Hohenstaufen, 1254-1268

Sixth Crusade, 1248-1254

Charles of Anjou (claimant), 1268

Seventh Crusade, 1270

APPENDIX V

PRINCES AND KINGS OF CILICIAN ARMENIA

RUBENID DYNASTY

Ruben I, 1080-1095
Constantine I (son), 1095-1099
T'oros (Theodore) I (son), 1100-1129
Levon (Leo) I (brother), 1129-1138
Cilicia occupied by the Byzantines, 1138-1145
T'oros (Theodore) II (son), 1145-1169
Ruben II (son), 1169-1170
Mleh (uncle), 1170-1175
Ruben III (nephew), 1175-1186
Levon (Leo) II (I) the Great (brother), 1186-1198/99; King of Armenia, 1198/99-1219
Isabel (daughter), 1219-1222
Philip of Antioch (consort), 1222-1225

HET'UMID DYNASTY

Het'um I of Lambron (second consort of Isabel), 1226-1269
Levon (Leo) III (II) (son), 1269-1289
Het'um II (son), 1289-1293, 1294-1296, 1299-1305
T'oros (Theodore) III (I) (brother), 1293-1294, d. 1299
Smbat (brother), 1296-1298
Constantine II (I) (brother), 1298-1299
Levon (Leo) IV (III) (son of T'oros III), 1305-1308
Oshin (son of Leo III), 1308-1320
Levon (Leo) V (IV) (son), 1320-1341

APPENDIX V

PRINCES AND KINGS OF CILICIAN ARMENIA

LUSIGNAN DYNASTY

Guy I de Lusignan
 (cousin of Leo V), 1342-1344;
 Regent: John de Lusignan
  (brother), 1342

Constantine III (II) (outsider),
 1344-1363

Constantine IV (III) (cousin),
 1365-1373

Peter de Lusignan, King of Cyprus,
 invited, 1368-1369

Leo VI (V) de Lusignan,
 (Guy's nephew), 1373-1375

Mamluk conquest of Cilician Armenia

Index

Abaqa Khan, 54; 57-59; 61-67; 80.

Abkhazia, 13; 25; 82.

Aghuan, 12; 25; 121.

Aleppo, 19; 30; 53-54; 59; 88; 102-103.

Alexander (the Great), 8; 12; 32; 39; 82.

Antioch, 5; 19; 23; 27-28; 53-54; 58; 75; 89; 108.

Arabia, 19; 20; 30; 87.

Arabic, 4; 11; 15; 20.

Arghun Khan, 65-68.

Armenia, 10-13; 16-19; 23; 25; 29; 46-49; 53-54; 57; 59-65; 67; 70; 72; 74-80; 89; 102-103; 105-108; 111; 119-121; 123-124.

Assyria(n), 20; 50.

Baghdad, 15; 25; 31; 47-48; 50-52; 70.

Baibars, 59; 89; 100.

Baiju, 40-41; 44; 48; 119; 122.

Barley, 4; 9.

Baidu, 68-70; 74-76.

Bedouins, 72; 87; 99; 109.

Beijing, 42; 81.

Berke Khan, 31; 55-57.

Bethlehem, 3; 115.

Butter, 9.

Byzantine, 88; 120.

Byzantium, 14.

Cairo, 85; 90-93; 103.

Caliph, 25-27; 47-48; 51; 88.

Camel, 85; 93; 101; 122.

Cappadocia, 17; 24.

Caspian Sea, 5-7; 10; 12; 119-121.

Cathay, 1-3; 42; 81; 115; 123.

Cattle, 1; 83; 93.

Caucasian Albanian (see Aghuan).

Caucasus, 6; 12; 39.

Chaldea, 15; 23-26.

Chingiz Khan, 32-38.

Cilicia, 17; 19; 24; 27; 57; 59; 120.

Constantinople, 18; 24; 27.

Copper, 17.

Copts, 93.

Cyprus, 17; 24; 41; 75; 80; 102-103; 107; 115.

Damascus, 19; 31; 54; 62; 70; 73-78; 89-90; 109-110.

Dokuz (khatun), 52.

Edward I, 88.

Egypt, 19; 54; 57-65; 70; 72-73; 75-76; 79; 85; 87-93; 97-101; 103-104; 110.

Erzurum, 40.

INDEX

Georgia, 13; 17; 25; 29; 40; 57; 63; 65; 67; 70; 78; 105.
Germany, 44.
Greece, 14; 17-18; 28.
Godfrey of Bouillon, 28-29; 31; 107.
Gold, 2; 8; 17; 51; 115.

Hamshen, 13.
Heraclius, 23; 27.

Isfahan, 10.

Jacobites, 18-20; 93.
Jerusalem, 15; 19-20; 30; 53-54; 74; 88; 93; 101; 109-110.
Jochi, 43; 45.

Kipchak (see Qipchaq).
Kitbuqa, 54-57; 89-91.
Komans, 44; 88-91; 100.
Konya, 17.
Kumis, 4.
Kurds, 11; 16; 61; 88.

Malik Shah I, 28-29.
Maronite(s), 20.
Media, 10-12; 15; 23; 26; 55-56; 88.
Mediterranean Sea, 17; 92.

Melitene, 102-103.
Mesopotamia, 16; 19; 24; 27-28; 72; 75; 103.
Mongke Khan, 42; 46; 49-50; 119; 121-124.
Milk, 4; 9; 83; 122.
Mosul, 16.
Mount Lebanon, 20; 72; 87; 104; 109.

Nestorian, 15; 20.
Nile river, 92-93; 101.
Nineveh, 15; 768.
North Africa, 92; 107.

Olive oil, 1.

Palestine, 19; 30; 55-57.
Parrots, 9.
Persia, 4; 7-12; 14; 23-26; 28-30; 43; 49-50; 54-55; 64; 74; 81.

Qipchaq, 70; 74-75; 81; 89; 100.
Qutlugh, 74-78.
Qutuz (Kutuz), 57; 89; 100.

Russia, 6; 44; 58.

Saladin, 88.

INDEX

Sarai, 7.

Shapur II, 13.

Sinjar (Mount), 16.

Smbat sparapet, 46; 115; 119.

Syriac, 15.

Tabriz, 12; 30; 54-55; 65-66; 81; 122.

Trabzon, 18.

Tripoli, 72; 89; 104; 107; 109.

Turkmen, 26-27; 87; 99; 107-109.

Uighurs, 3.

Wheat, 1; 3-5; 9.

Wine, 3-5; 17.

Yazdegerd III, 24.

www.sophenearmenianlibrary.com

www.ingramcontent.com/pod-product-compliance
Lightning Source LLC
Chambersburg PA
CBHW030301100526
44590CB00012B/478